History & Guide

Chesterfield

Geoff Sadler

To Mary

Best Wishes
Geoff Sadler.
9 · 1 · 02

Band concert in the park, early in the twentieth century. The bandstand shown, which dated from the 1890s, was later dismantled and replaced by the present structure in 1923. The venue for a range of social and sporting events, Queen's Park is still Chesterfield's main leisure facility.

History & Guide

Chesterfield

Geoff Sadler

'They were to go no further northward than Derbyshire. In that county there
was enough to be sure to occupy the chief of their three weeks.'
Jane Austen, *Pride and Prejudice*

'However, from an attentive survey of Derbyshire we shall find, that the state
of the county at this distant period is not involved entirely in darkness.'
James Pilkington, *A View of the Present State of Derbyshire,* 1789

'Chesterfield is a large but irregularly built town, pleasantly situated between
two rivulets, the Hyper and Rother, in the beautiful and fertile vale of
Scarsdale, and is the second considerable town in the county of Derby. The
Saxon name of Chester proves it to be a place of great antiquity, and it is
imagined to have originated in a Roman station.'
J. Pigot & Co., *London & Provincial New Commercial Directory,* 1822-23

TEMPUS

Tempus Publishing Limited
The Mill, Brimscombe Port,
Stroud, Gloucestershire, GL5 2QG

ISBN 0 7524 2451 3

Typesetting and origination by
Tempus Publishing Limited
Printed in Great Britain by
Midway Colour Print, Wiltshire

Queen's Park dedication, September 1887. Founded in tribute to Queen Victoria's Golden Jubilee, Queen's Park was formally dedicated in 1887, when a procession of tableaux demonstrating local trades moved through the park. This photograph by A. Seaman & Sons shows a blacksmith at work, and the man standing in the foreground is Mr C.E. Jones, Secretary of the Queen's Park Committee.

CONTENTS

PREFACE & ACKNOWLEDGMENTS

Since the Romans first arrived here in Nero's day, Chesterfield has undergone many startling changes, and with the passing of time these have become more frequent and rapid. The last few years have seen the town transformed, with familiar landmarks removed to be replaced by bright new shopping and leisure centres and superstores. This process of change is set to continue as the town finds a new role for itself in the third millennium.

This book documents some of these changes, and celebrates the many different 'stars' Chesterfield has produced in its past. Most people know about George Stephenson and Bob Wilson, but how many are aware that this town can lay claim to a Nobel Prize-winner, a recipient of the Victoria Cross, an Archbishop of Canterbury, a Mayor of New York and a Lord Mayor of London, a Speaker of the House of Commons and the designer of 'the best amateur observatory in the country'? These, and others, are due for an appearance in the following pages. While I cannot claim to describe Chesterfield's past in every detail – even the official history of five large volumes doesn't manage this, going no further forward than 1939 – I can certainly promise to include some aspects not met with in previous works, together with a few images not seen before.

Sincere thanks to Brian Austin for his help and advice, and to Brian Davis for the scanning of over 100 images, and for some excellent original photographs. Thanks also go to Derbyshire Library Service for permission to use images from Chesterfield Library's collection, to my colleagues Ann Krawszik, Diane Bennell, Susan Bradley and Patrick Scott for loan of original photographs, and to Jacqui Barnett and Keith Jacques for images from the late Fred Jacques' collection; to Mrs G. M. Wilsher for permission to reproduce photographs by her late husband R. Wilsher; to Peter Sutherland of Walton Lodge, Sonia Preece and Spital History Group, Dennis Denton and the Chesterfield Astronomical Society, Philip Riden, George Martin, John Stanley, and two photographers sadly no longer with us, Derek Jones and Roy Stafford; to C.H. Nadin, Seaman & Sons, Jackson's bakers, Diane Naylor and Chatsworth House, Melanie Blake and Courtauld Institute of Art, Peter White and Robinson & Sons, Anne-Marie Knowles and Chesterfield Borough Museum, Chesterfield Borough Council, Mike Wilson and the *Derbyshire Times*; my colleague Alun Waterhouse for his generous technical assistance, and to the Ordnance Survey for permission to reproduce old series maps. Finally, many thanks to Charlotte Christensen and Tempus Publishing for thinking of me as the author of this work, and for their help in bringing it about.

The following list is of books that give further information on Chesterfield and its history. All items are available for loan or consultation in the Chesterfield Local Studies Library.

Becket, J.V. and Polack, J.P. 'The Scarsdale Surveys of 1652-62', in *A Seventeenth Century Scarsdale Miscellany*, Derbyshire Record Society, 1993

Bestall, J. M., and others, *The History of Chesterfield*, Chesterfield Borough Council (5 volumes):
    Vol. 1, *Early & Medieval Chesterfield*, edited J.M. Bestall, C.B.C. 1974
    Vol. 2, Part 1. *Tudor & Stuart Chesterfield*, edited Philip Riden, C.B.C. 1984
    Vol. 2, Part 2. *Restoration & Georgian Chesterfield*, edited J.M. Bestall & D.V. Fowkes, C.B.C. 1984
    Vol. 3. *Early Victorian Chesterfield*, edited J.M. Bestall, C.B.C. 1978
    Vol. 4. *The Development of the Modern Town: 1851-1939*, edited T.F. Wright, C.B.C. 1992
    Vol. 5. *Records of the Borough of Chesterfield*, edited Philip Riden & John Blair, C.B.C. 1980

Cooper, Roy, *The Book of Chesterfield*, Barracuda, 1977

Ford, Thomas, *History of Chesterfield*, Ford, 1839

Godfrey, W.E., 'The Plague of Chesterfield 1586-7', *Derbyshire Archaeological Journal* Vol. 74, 1954

Foster, Albert J., *Round About the Crooked Spire*, Chapman & Hall, 1894

Hardy, C., *Francis Frith's Around Chesterfield*, Frith Book Co., 1999

Hall, Revd George, *History of Chesterfield*, 1823

Hart, C.R., *North Derbyshire Archaeological Survey to AD 1500*, N.D.A.T., 1981

Hirst, John, *Chesterfield Breweries*, Hirst, 1991

Martin, G.W., *More Memories of Chesterfield*, True North, 2000

Monet-Lane, H.C., *The Romans in Chesterfield*, Lane, 1985

Pendleton, John, and W. Jacques, *Modern Chesterfield*, Derbyshire Courier, 1903

Richardson, Christine, *Minutes of the Chesterfield Canal Company 1771-1780*, edited by Philip Riden, Derbyshire Records Society, 1996

Riden, Philip, 'Some Unpublished Roman Discoveries near Chesterfield', *Derbyshire Archaeological Journal* Vol. 100, 1980

Smith, Mark, *Memories of Chesterfield*, True North, 1998

Thompson, Roy, *Chesterfield* (Archive Photographs Series), Chalford, 1994

Thompson, Roy, *Chesterfield 1945-1995* (Archive Photographs Series), Chalford, 1996

Thompson, Roy, and Lilley, John, *Chesterfield in old picture postcards*, European Library, 1989

White, Peter, *From Pillboxes to Bandages and Back Again: the Robinson Story 1839-2000*, Robinson & Sons Ltd, 2000

For readers wishing to discover more about Chesterfield:

Chesterfield Borough Museum, St Mary's Gate

Formerly the Stephenson Memorial Hall and home of the public library, the museum was opened in 1994 by television antiques expert Henry Sandon. It holds a variety of artefacts including Roman and medieval finds and items relating to George Stephenson, early railways and local industries. As well as permanent displays on the theme of 'The Story of Chesterfield', the museum also runs a series of regular exhibitions. Some local history publications are available for sale.

Hours: Mon, Tues, Thurs, Fri, Sat 10-4 (including Bank Holidays). Admission free. Chesterfield Museum, St Mary's Gate, Chesterfield, S41 7TY Tel: 01246 345727

The Peacock Information & Heritage Centre on Low Pavement

A listed building dating from 1500 and formerly a guildhall and inn, the centre provides heritage and tourist information on seasonal activities and events in and around Chesterfield. Regular exhibitions are held in the centre, and well dressings take place annually in the old inn yard at the rear of the building. Some local history publications are available for sale.

Hours: Mon-Sat 11-4. Admission free. Peacock Heritage & Information Centre, Low Pavement, Chesterfield Tel: 01246 345777/8

Chesterfield Library, New Beetwell Street

Opened by Mark Fisher MP in 1985, the library has won the R.I.B.A. & the T.C. Farries/You & Yours awards. The Local Studies Library holds a comprehensive collection of books on Chesterfield history, as well as a number of original theses and manuscript items. Also in the collection are 4,000 maps (the earliest dating back to 1577), and over 17,000 photographs. Local newspapers from 1732 to date are available on microfilm, and the library offers internet access to local and family history sources. Some local history publications are available for sale.

Hours: Mon-Fri 9.30-7; Sat 9.30-4. Admission free (charge for internet use only). Chesterfield Library, New Beetwell Street, Chesterfield, S40 1QN Tel: 01246 209292

CHAPTER 1

Signs of Life

To begin with, there was no Chesterfield. Only a gently rising stretch of land on the southern slope of a hill overlooking the rivers later known as the Rother and the Hipper in their valley beneath. As far as we can tell, this spur of ground remained uninhabited through the Stone Age period, by which time early man had established himself in the caves of Creswell Crags a few miles further east. For some time after that, it left no record of other visitors, although flint implements and a waste blade found in later years in the clay ramparts of the excavated Roman fort offer the tantalising possibility of Bronze Age inhabitants.

The first occupants appear to have been Iron Age settlers, who at least left some trace behind them. In the course of a series of archaeological excavations in Church Lane and the Alpine Gardens from 1973 to 1975, H.C. Monet-Lane uncovered evidence of a pre-Roman Iron Age structure that had subsequently been destroyed. Not a hill fort to match the Peak District strongholds of Carl Wark or Bakewell further west, but rather a fortified homestead, it extended only a short distance; it was later covered over by Woolworth's store and is now part of a busy shopping area. Not too surprisingly, its demolition coincided with the arrival of the next long-term tenants, the Romans.

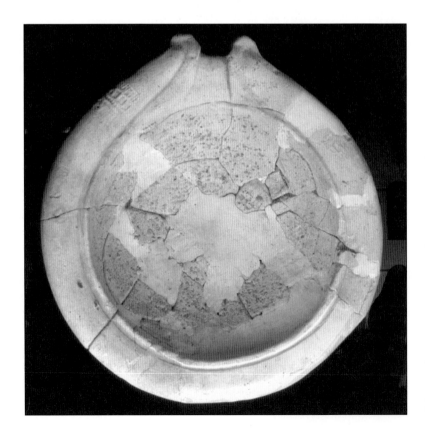

A Roman mortarium *from the late first century, a vessel used for grinding food. On display in Chesterfield Museum.*

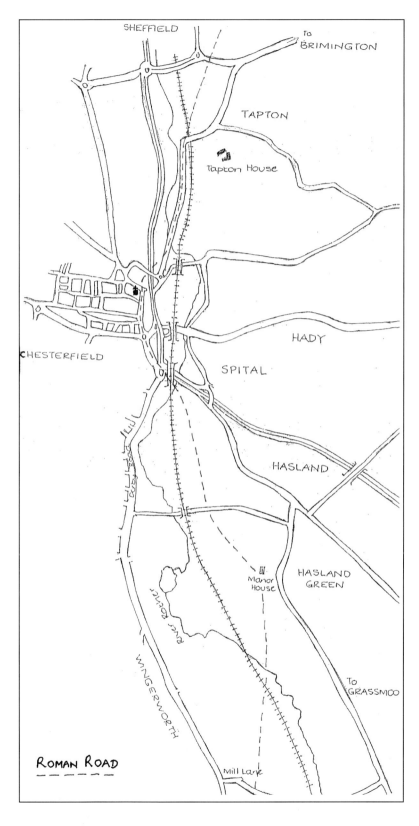

SHEFFIELD

To
BRIMINGTON

TAPTON

Tapton House

CHESTERFIELD

HADY

SPITAL

HASLAND

HASLAND
GREEN

Manor
House

To
GRASSMOO

WINGERWORTH

RIVER ROTHER

DERBY ROAD

Mill Lane

ROMAN ROAD

Map showing the likely route of Ryknield Street, the Roman road running north from Derby to Templeborough, of which the fortified camp at Chesterfield formed a part. The road is thought to have run north from Mill Lane, Wingerworth, crossing the Rother at Hasland Green before turning north-west by Hasland Manor to follow the route of the modern A617 into Chesterfield via Lordsmill Street/St Mary's Gate.

When the Romans reached what is now Chesterfield, they were moving north from Derby along the military road that eventually ran through to their fort at Templeborough, a road later to be known as Ryknield Street. The direction of their route has been confirmed as far as Mill Lane at Wingerworth. After that opinions differ, and most of the evidence has been wiped out by later industrial development, but Riden and others have been able to put a strong case for an advance north-east to Hasland Green, crossing the Rother and moving north-west through Storforth Lane and the Horn's Bridge area to the lower end of Lordsmill Street, and on into the town along St Mary's Gate. This certainly fits the layout of the Chesterfield fort; further corroboration is provided by the discovery of what were probably Roman road surfaces at Horn's Bridge during reconstruction work in 1932, and a similar find of a Roman roadway at the Eastwood Wagon Works on Brimington Road in 1866. Contrary to a belief commonly held at one time, the road did not take in the now vanished earthwork known as Tapton Castle and erroneously claimed as a Roman fortification. This particular 'castle' was a medieval construction, and has no real connection with Roman Chesterfield.

Chesterfield was then a frontier territory, within the border region between two Celtic peoples, the subjugated Coritani and their powerful northern neighbours, the Brigantes. Exactly where the tribal frontier lay has again been argued. Most historians favour the Chesterfield site as lying within Brigantian territory, although Monet-Lane for one argues otherwise. What mattered was that the Romans were quick to spot the advantages it offered. Here they had a clear vantage point with a view of the river valleys and the immediate surrounding area, and the confluence of the Hipper and Rother (a name derived from a Celtic word meaning 'great river') provided access to fresh water. Its strategic location virtually in the centre of Britain made it a useful link with other legionary forts, and provided a starting-point for movement westward into the Peak District with its lucrative lead-mines while at the same time protecting the northern road and keeping an eye on the hostile Brigantes.

They took possession of their new home, settling at what is now the southern part of the town and raising their own fortified enclosure to supersede the Iron Age settlement, now destroyed. A succession of archaeological excavations in our own time have confirmed the fact of their occupation. H.C. Monet-Lane explored the Alpine Gardens and Church Lane between 1973 and 1975, T.W. Courtney supervised further operations in Spa Lane, Swan Yard and Station Road from 1974 to 1978, and more recently a University of Manchester archaeological unit made an extensive search of the large vicarage garden between Church Lane and Vicar Lane prior to its obliteration by the new Vicar Lane retail development. Their combined efforts have revealed the remains of a Roman military settlement, with traces of ditch and rampart together with brooches, coins, and fragments of pottery and glass, finds described as being 'of the highest calibre'. The fortification would appear to have covered the area bounded by Stephenson Place and Church Way to the west and south, and by Holywell Street and Station Road to the north and east. It is the area since occupied by the parish church, and which forms the core of the later medieval town.

The fortified camp made by the Romans was not built in a single attempt, but in several distinct phases over the better part of a century. Evidence from the digs shows that the original fort was erected around AD 54-55, at a time when the Romans had begun their gradual pacification of the Brigantes further north. Later on a ditch was dug to the south-east, and further timber buildings were raised, while later still a larger ditch was added to the south, which was afterwards filled in. The fort was rebuilt around AD 100 with an eastern entrance on Station Road and with the south-east corner near the junction with Spa Lane. Excavation has revealed that in the time that followed ovens and furnaces were used there, probably for metal-working. By AD 140 the fort was abandoned, but although not subsequently used by a military garrison, finds in the churchyard and town centre show that some Romano-British people were living there in the second and third centuries. Finds from the latter stages of occupation include imported Samian pottery, a luxury item from Gaul, which suggests these Cestrefeldians enjoyed a comfortable lifestyle for their time.

What do we know about the Romans in Chesterfield? What kind of people were they? When the first soldiers arrived, in the reign of the Emperor Nero, they were probably the foot-slogging legionaries who made up the backbone of the Roman military machine. No proof exists to show whether Chesterfield was a legionary fortress, or one garrisoned by auxiliary troops. If these early inhabitants of Chesterfield were legionaries, they may have been Italians, or possibly Spaniards (the IX Hispana was one of the legions in Britain at the time); if auxiliaries, they could have come from almost any corner of the known world. They may have been Gauls or Germans, local British levies, or even Arabs or Turco-Mongolian Scyths from Asia. During their hundred years of occupation garrisons would have been added to or replaced, and we can safely assume that by the time they left they would have been a far more racially mixed bunch. It is most unlikely they would have lived a monastic life. Then, as now, soldiers would find female companions, and the indications of civilian settlement suggest the possibility of British wives, girlfriends and children. What happened to them when the Romans marched away remains an open question, but the chances are that several Coritanian or Brigantian ladies were left literally 'holding the baby'.

By AD 140 both soldiers and civilians were gone, the fortified camp left to moulder as it fell prey to the ravages of time and weather. The Romans in Chesterfield came, saw and conquered, but within a century they had marched away. In the end their most enduring memorial is in the name of the town that sprang up after they had left. The 'Chester' in 'Chesterfield' comes from the Latin *castra* (fortified camp) and is the one part of their legacy familiar to us today.

What happened next we are none too sure. With Britain largely pacified by this time, the Roman departure was probably because Chesterfield had outlived its usefulness, rather than because of any threat from the largely Romanised native peoples. Their rule in Britain would last another three centuries, until the withdrawal of the legions and the incursions of new and more savage invaders along the eastern coast. As yet, the earth of Chesterfield gives us no answers. The Roman departure leaves the way open for a time of turmoil and war, but also of new beginnings: a period we have called the Dark Ages.

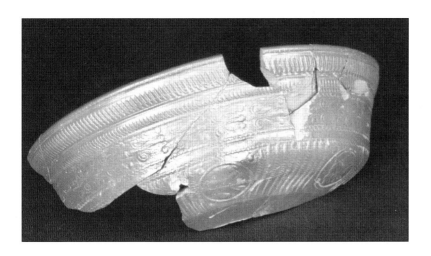

An example of Samian ware displayed in Chesterfield Museum. Imported from Roman Gaul, this was a luxury item, and suggests a comfortable lifestyle for some of Chesterfield's early inhabitants.

CHAPTER 2

Dark Age to Domesday

By the time the Romans left Britain, their island province had come under sustained attack from seafaring German invaders. The newcomers formed the western spearhead of successive waves of migrating nations who for centuries had flooded against the strained frontiers of the Roman empire until these had at last given way. Now, with the power of Rome at an end, these men and women reached the edge of the European continent, and looked beyond to Britain for their new homeland.

The names that have come down to us – Angles, Saxons and Jutes – are convenient labels for several related peoples whose main bond was their Germanic origin and their need for living-space. Their language would later be adopted as English, and as such become the national tongue of the conquered island, renamed England after the Anglian invaders. They landed along the eastern coasts, and within a generation they were in effective control of the country, the Romanised British defeated and driven back into remote enclaves to form new kingdoms. Anglian settlers penetrated what is now Derbyshire from the south, moving north along the Trent valley to reach the decayed Roman settlement perhaps as late as AD 600. We say perhaps because archaeology has as yet found no definite answers. That they farmed the land round about seems plain from neighbouring districts whose names end in 'ton', from the Old English *tun* (farm). Whittington, Brimington and Tapton are three examples of Anglian farmsteads that later grew into independent villages. What the newcomers made of Chesterfield we cannot be sure. It is possible, as historian J.M. Bestall has suggested, that some traces of the fortified camp remained and were noted by the Anglian settlers, whether or not they made use of the site. The fact that they were later to include the Roman element in their name for the town certainly shows the place was known to them.

Their search for suitable land accomplished, the Angles settled down to a – mainly peaceful – agricultural existence. The arrival in Repton of St Aidan in AD 653 brought the return of Christianity to England, and the new religion was gradually adopted by the pagan English, proving a civilising influence on the descendants of the former 'sea-wolves'. Chesterfield and its region found themselves part of the Anglo-Saxon kingdom of Mercia, which covered most of the modern Midlands, although in keeping with their earlier frontier status between Brigantes and Coritani they were now close to Mercia's border with its northern neighbour Northumbria.

All too soon the English, now a settled and Christian people, were obliged to face another wave of seaborne invasions from fierce pagan warriors, the Vikings of Scandinavia. Beginning with a series of bloody raids at the tail-end of the eighth century, the onslaught reached its climax in 867 when a large Danish army captured York and established its base there. Moving south, the Danes overran Mercia and East Anglia, and were checked only after some hard campaigning by Alfred of Wessex. Following his treaty with the Danish leader Guthrum, Chesterfield became part of another frontier between the Anglo-Saxon kingdoms and the Viking region known as the Danelaw, centred on the 'five boroughs' of Nottingham, Derby, Leicester, Lincoln and Stamford.

A tenth-century Scandinavian silver ingot found at Temple Normanton in 1998. Though unprepossessing, this is a rare reminder that Chesterfield once lay on the frontier of Danish occupation. Now in the British Museum.

A pagan people with a mainly oral literature, the Scandinavians have left as sparse a record here as the early English invaders. A silver ingot found in nearby Temple Normanton in 1998, which was identified as tenth-century Scandinavian, is virtually the only hard archaeological find from this period, and once again it is local place-names that provide any evidence of their stay. The districts of Boythorpe (*thorp*, Scandinavian, small settlement) and Birdholme (*holm*, Scandinavian, island) are two examples, while Normanton (later Temple Normanton) means 'farm of the Norwegians'. Scandinavian names also survive in the administrative division of Scarsdale (Norse, 'Skarf's valley'), an area covering Chesterfield and most of north-east Derbyshire. Scarsdale was described as a 'wapentake', another Viking term referring to a ceremonial hosting of armed warriors. The word 'wapentake' was replaced only centuries later by the Old English 'hundred', and even today people still refer to 'the Scarsdale hundred'. A further development came with the dividing of the country into shires, and Chesterfield now became part of Derbyshire.

The eventual defeat of the Danes and the reconquest of their territories by Alfred and his descendants returned control of the country to the native English, and over the following centuries Anglo-Saxon civilisation thrived and flourished. It is during this period that Chesterfield is first mentioned by name, in a document of AD 955 where King Eadred gives to the Mercian nobleman Uhtred Child 'the grant of land at Chesterfield forever' and 'the freedom to build a town and bridge'. Chesterfield appears in the grant as 'Cesterfelda', meaning open country near the Roman fortification or camp. From this point onwards, it enters recorded history, although how far Uhtred got with his building is open to question. If any settlement resulted, it must have been on a very small scale, and once again there is no real archaeological proof.

Relations with Scandinavia remained tense. The great battle of Brunanburh, where Alfred's grandson Athelstan routed an army of Scots and Irish Vikings in 937, may have taken place only a few miles north of Chesterfield, at Brinsworth in the vicinity of Rotherham, but the location of the battle is fiercely contested by historians. In 1016, invasion brought a Danish king (Canute) to the throne, but his rule endured for little more than a generation. He was not to have the impact of the invaders who

Map drawn in 1801 by Charles Smith, indicating the tribal territories of the Coritani and Brigantes, and the Anglo-Scandinavian Scarsdale wapentake or hundred.

came after him, from across the Channel. The year 1066 saw the battle of Hastings, and the utter defeat and humiliation of the English by the mailed cavalry of the Normans, a dynamic and ruthless people whose blood mixed French with Viking ancestry.

Under the leadership of Duke William, who after Hastings was renamed 'the Conqueror' (more flattering than his previous title of 'the Bastard'), these new masters were to reshape the face of England, and with it the future of Chesterfield itself.

A Town Takes Shape: the Middle Ages

With William the Conqueror on the throne, England entered a new era of authoritarian rule as a feudal, centralized state. William himself embodied the Norman philosophy. A severe taskmaster and merciless to his enemies, he was also a skilled organizer who rewarded loyalty in his followers. His reign saw a great building programme of castles and churches, whose appearance served to emphasize the close relationship between Norman church and state. It was inevitable that the *Domesday Book*, that unique combination of census and account-ledger of 1086, should have been compiled at his command. It is in the *Domesday Book* that we hear of Chesterfield for a second time. Under the heading 'The Land of the King' and 'Scarvedele (Scarsdale) Wapentake' is the following passage:

'Manor. In Nevvebold with six berewites, Witintune, Brimintune, Tapetune, Cestrefeld, Buitorp, Echintune, there are six carucates and one ox-gang of land for geld. Land for six ploughs. The King has sixteen villanes and two bordars and one serf there having four ploughs. To this manor belong eight acres of meadow. Wood, pasturable, three miles in length and three miles in breadth. In the time of King Edward it was worth six pounds; now, ten pounds.'

So Chesterfield appears once more, having made the change from English Cesterfelda to Norman Cestrefeld, as one of six beriwicks of the manor of Newbold. (A 'beriwick' was a hamlet of a manor or lordship, but separated from it.) Much has since been made of the apparent pre-eminence of Newbold at this time, but probably all that it signifies is that the Normans had erected a hall here to serve as their administrative headquarters ('Newbold', a Norman word, means 'new building'). Certainly it is most unlikely that Newbold was any larger than the other places mentioned, most of which at this time would be little more than overgrown farmsteads. The immediate population of sixteen villeins (farmers), two bordars (smallholders) and a serf give us some idea of the numbers involved, and most historians suggest that no more than ninety people inhabited the entire manor. The value of the area is also interesting, having increased from £6 to £10 since William's occupation of the throne. Bearing in mind the savage 'harrying of the north' not long before in 1069-70, when rebellion had been put down with brutal punishments and a scorched-earth policy, Chesterfield seems to have differed from its neighbours, prospering rather than suffering during the Conquest period.

Newbold's importance was to prove short-lived. Barely seven years later, in 1093, the son of the Conqueror reversed his decision. William II, better known as 'Rufus', presented Chesterfield as a separate manor to the Dean of Lincoln. It is ironic that Chesterfield should benefit from two of our least popular medieval kings. William Rufus granted Chesterfield its independence from Newbold, a status it was to retain. Here, from modest beginnings, we are able to trace the growth of Chesterfield as a medieval market town. Over a century later the even less loved King John, in his charter of 1204, enabled William Brewer to lay out the framework of the town we know today.

It grew from the southern edge of the modern town from the core area around today's parish church, in a grid of streets, most of which are still with us, some bearing the Scandinavian suffix 'gate' (from *gata*, street). Saltergate, the main thoroughfare through the centre of Chesterfield, is an obvious example and, in common with most of the town's medieval streets, is thought to take its name from the trade practised there.

Routes had already been established for the transport of salt from the Cheshire mines further west, and, like the fleeces from the later medieval boom in wool, it came across the Pennines and down through the Peak by packhorse and along Saltergate into the town. Running parallel to Saltergate came a later arrival, Knifesmithgate, and crossing between the two was Glumangate (from 'gleeman', minstrel), while beyond the church ran Holywell Street (originally Haliwelegate). The last is believed to have been named after a holy well dedicated to St Helen, the canonized mother of Constantine, Rome's first Christian emperor, and alleged discoverer of a piece from Christ's cross. The name of St Helen survives in our own time as a street and an electoral ward in the town.

Another more mysterious street was Soutergate, street of the shoemakers, which was later to become St Mary's Gate and Lordsmill Street. The Shambles, adjoining the modern market place, is also of medieval origin (one of its alleys, Packer's Row, suggests the old packhorse routes), and was itself the place where animals were slaughtered. Apparently the natural slope allowed the blood of the butchered

A reconstruction of medieval Chesterfield by Philip Riden, showing the church, the sites of the Old and New Market Places, and the layout of the principal streets by William Brewer after 1204.

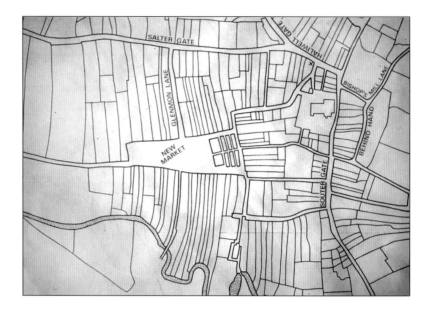

creatures to run down into the Hipper below. Its name comes from 'Flesh-charnels' or 'Flesh-shambles', later corrupted to 'Fleshamols' and ultimately to 'Shambles'.

The historian Philip Riden has researched the origins of Chesterfield's medieval streets, and his reconstructed map gives an excellent picture of the town's layout at this time. From the street-names alone it becomes clear that Chesterfield now had its own local industries and trades. Cloth was being produced and dyed there, and shoemaking and the tanning of leather had particular prominence in the town. Corn was ground at the Bishop's Mill and the Lord's Mill, both of which gave their names to the streets on which they stood. Lordsmill Street, which was given in its name in a later century, still leads into Chesterfield from the south-east, but Bishop Mill Lane, which stood off Station Road until the early nineteenth century, has since disappeared.

Within 200 years of William Rufus's decree, Chesterfield was in business as a thriving, bustling medieval town. By our own standards it was still a small place, and would remain so until relatively modern times, but in medieval eyes it had considerable importance as a centre for local trading routes, and a hive of local industry. It also had a number of unusual visitors. The Royal Oak in the Shambles occupies the site of a much older inn that played host to members of the Templar order, who presumably stopped off in Chesterfield on journeys to or from their settlement at nearby Temple Normanton. The Templars were a knightly order founded in the Holy Land, and their presence reminds us that this was the time of the Crusades, and that Derbyshire people may well have fought and died in battles in faraway lands across the sea. It is easy to imagine the tall tales that some of them might have told on their return, and how their audience must have listened awe-stricken at the wonders they described. Unfortunately, such travels had their downside, and one of the less welcome gifts the returning crusaders brought was the scourge of leprosy. St Leonard's leper hospital was founded late in the twelfth century, at the foot of Hady Hill. At that time it was a safe distance from the medieval town, although it now forms part of a built-up area. The district of Spital takes its name from the leper hospital, long since vanished, and St Leonard again survives as an electoral ward. More recently, in June 2000, a skeleton was discovered in a garden on Picadilly Road and identified as a medieval priest from the twelfth century. He too is thought to have been associated with St Leonard's hospital.

From contemporary documents we learn that the hospital was funded with money from markets and fairs in the town, evidence of Chesterfield's thriving commercial state at this time. The original market, in existence before the end of the twelfth century, lay to the north of the parish church and south of Holywell Street. A small area that left no room for further development, it was superseded after 1204 by a larger market on the western side of the town, with the area that later became the Shambles a feature on the market's eastern edge. Although it was to become famous as the workplace of butchers, in those early days other tradesmen were operating there, as is clear from the names of the alleys or rows, such as Draper's Row or Mercer's Row. Both markets continued for a time, the older one being used for the smaller Tuesday market day while the main event on Saturdays was held on the newer, larger site. Eventually the new market took over and, with some slight alteration, is the one familiar to today's inhabitants.

King John's charter of 1204 granted to William Brewer 'the manor of Chesterfield, with Brimington and Whittington and the soke, and the whole wapentake of Scarsdale'. Formerly the property of the king himself, Chesterfield was now, under the lordship of Brewer, proclaimed to be a 'free borough', one of a handful of such towns in the country at that time. Furthermore, the burgesses were allowed to hold weekly markets on Tuesdays and Saturdays, and an eight-day fair every year on the Feast of the Holy Rood on 14 September, and they enjoyed 'the same liberties as the borough of Nottingham'. Given the size of Chesterfield compared to the much larger Nottingham, the charter was an impressive gift, and the markets and fairs were a useful source of income to the already wealthy lord of the manor.

A royal holding from the time of Domesday, Chesterfield now passed from a king to his favoured retainer William Brewer, a formidable and charismatic figure who might well be described as Chesterfield's original 'godfather'. A powerful landowner with estates in his native Devonshire as well as the Chesterfield manor, he was adviser to four Plantaganet kings, and a strong supporter of royal authority against the barons. Brewer negotiated Richard the Lionheart's release from captivity, and was later the right-hand man of his less popular brother John. The latter, recognizing Brewer's value to the crown, created him Sheriff of Derbyshire and Nottinghamshire, and it is easy to visualize Brewer as the model for the legendary 'Sheriff of Nottingham' in the Robin Hood ballads that sprang up a hundred years later in the neighbouring counties of Yorkshire and Nottinghamshire. It was he who supervised the layout of the medieval town, an ambitious task which established the grid-iron pattern of its early streets and the central Market Place that was then one of the largest in the country.

Like most land-owning barons of his time, Brewer was a ruthless, acquisitive man who amassed wealth and property during his long career. On the other hand, he was clearly a valued adviser to successive kings, and his long-term overlordship of Chesterfield proved a stabilizing influence. The Middle Ages were a violent, disruptive time where might was all too often right, and power struggles between barons and kings would continue for centuries, culminating in the bloody Wars of the Roses. After the death of Brewer and his heirs, lordship of the manor passed to the Wake family through marriage to Brewer's daughter Isabel. The Wakes were themselves great landowners, with estates in other counties, but their tenure of Chesterfield did not remain untroubled. Baldwin Wake joined the rebellion of the barons against Henry III, and the result was the Battle of Chesterfield in 1266.

Having destroyed the main rebel army led by his popular and dangerous rival Simon de Montfort at the battle of Evesham the year before, the King determined to settle accounts with the Midland barons. A royal army led by the king's nephew, Henry of Almaine, advanced on Chesterfield to meet the rebels whose leader was Robert Ferrers, Earl of Derby. There are conflicting accounts of the action, including the possibility of an attack using covered wagons (shades of the Wild West!). Certainly the rebels were taken by surprise, and most of their leaders fled the field, the royal army winning a decisive victory. Precisely where the battle took place remains unclear, but the contemporary account, later revised by the Whittington antiquary Revd Samuel Pegge, indicates that Chesterfield residents were involved. It was Pegge's view that the fighting must have taken place near to the church. This seems to be confirmed by the fact that some locals, 'the men of Brampton', defended a wall there and refused admittance to any of the combatants, and also by the capture of the Earl of Derby, Robert Ferrers. Again, accounts of his capture differ, one claiming he was sick and had just been bled, and was therefore in no condition to resist. The other, more picturesque, version has him hiding among a heap of woolsacks in the church itself, where he is betrayed to the royalists by the treachery of a woman. Open to dispute, of course, but it makes a better story! As for Baldwin Wake, he went into hiding on the Isle of Axholme, but eventually surrendered and obtained pardon and restitution of his lands. Pegge remarks that: 'he lost the manor of Chesterfield, along with his other lands, for a time, which was seized by the king and his party; but, upon his submission, it was restored to him, and continued in his family for some time.' Ferrers, the ringleader, was less fortunate; imprisoned at Windsor, he was stripped of his estates and title.

Altogether more disturbing was the murderous violence that took place in and around the parish church on 1 January 1422. While mass was being sung, local landowners Thomas and Richard Foljambe and the chaplain Thomas Cokke led 200 armed Lancastrians in an attack on those inside the church. Their onslaught was carefully planned beforehand, and involved a treacherous parish clerk, who shut the doors of the belfry, vestry and crucifix chamber and then rang the church bells as a signal for the attack. The intruders pushed their way into the church, drawing their swords as they neared the font. The vicar, Richard Dawson, tried to intervene but was threatened by the Foljambes and their armed followers, and quickly withdrew to the altar. The Lancastrians then fell on their unprepared victims, and in the course of the assault four men – Henry Pierpoint, Henry Longford, William Bradshaw and Thomas Hasilby – had the thumbs hacked from their hands, wounds which disabled them from using their own weapons. Arrows were shot over the high altar, and the terrified vicar threw down the eucharist he was holding. Other wounds were dealt, and Pierpoint's servants also came under attack. The action ended in murder when Longford and Bradshaw were butchered, Bradshaw's death-wound a blow to the head that saw his blood and brains spilled near an altar of the Virgin. What price sanctuary, one wonders? Pierpoint was led outside, where a local merchant William Brampton urged that he be killed, but Richard Foljambe and Thomas Milne interceded for him, and the wretched man was left to go home 'bleeding and maimed'. Presumably Hasilby got home in a similar state, if he was lucky.

A month later a Derby jury decided that Thomas Foljambe and others were guilty of murder, but might remained right, and it was thirty years and more before the surviving murderers were brought to book. The ninety men still living in 1454 included thirteen Chesterfield people. They were imprisoned in the Marshalsea gaol pending trial, but history does not record what happened to them. It is possible they may never have paid for their crimes.

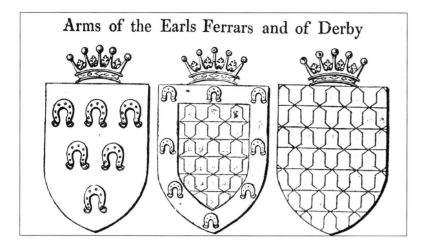

Arms of the Earls Ferrars and of Derby

Ferrers family arms. The Ferrers family, later Earls of Derby, were lords under William the Conqueror. Ralph Ferrers appears in the Domesday Book as manor lord of Newbold.

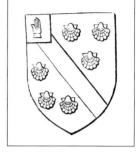

Foljambe family arms. The Foljambes of Walton were lords of the manor of Chesterfield and High Sheriffs of Derbyshire in the Middle Ages.

Peverel family arms. The Peverels, descendants of William the Conqueror by his natural son William Peverel, were founders of Peveril Castle at Castleton and of the original Bolsover Castle.

Even today, nearly 600 years after the event, the incident of 1 January 1422 has the power to shock the modern reader. The conniving of gentry and a clergyman with local officials to commit wounding and murder inside a church, the disregard of the right of sanctuary, the violent threats made to the vicar himself – all would certainly merit front-page news nowadays. Like so many other events of medieval and later times, it tells us that this was another, more brutal age, when force counted most, and when the law could be made to answer the needs of the rich and powerful.

This said, the power of the lords and their retainers did not pass unchallenged. The 'men of Chesterfield', the burgesses mentioned in King John's Charter of 1204 with its grant of land to William Brewer, were already beginning to assert themselves and secure rights of their own. These rights were given further support by a charter from John, son of Baldwin Wake, in 1294 'to his men of Chesterfield, holders of burgages… that they may enjoy the same liberties and free customs which they had by grant from William le Brewer'. This period saw the establishing of guilds in the town, notably the merchant guild, while the charter of 1294 entitled them to various privileges and to lay down restrictions regarding the local trades that were so vital to Chesterfield's development as a commercial centre. This early hint of 'restrictive practices' was balanced by the creation of guilds of a different kind, concerned with the social welfare and support of their members. The guild of St Helen, associated with St Helen's chapel on the Sheffield road, was one of several such organizations, while the later guild of the Blessed Mary (formed in 1392) had direct links with the parish church. As time went on, the leader of the guild, known as an 'alderman', came to be regarded as the chief citizen of the borough, and effectively ran Chesterfield with a council of twelve guild members. Then, as now, Chesterfield's overlords were 'absentees' with other estates, who did not

Leake family arms. The Leakes were the original owners of Sutton Scarsdale Hall, which, like Chesterfield, formed part of the Scarsdale hundred.

live in the town itself. Inevitably, they came to be regarded as interfering 'foreigners' putting obstacles in the way of commerce and profit. As time went on, the rights of 'the men of Chesterfield' and control of their town's prosperity became a legal battleground as they struggled to break free from the grip of the manor lords.

Medieval Chesterfield was a small settlement, its houses and workshops packed closely together in the network of streets around the parish church, surrounded by outlying crofts and field-strips, and with the market on its western edge. Few enough reminders are left us now from those far-off days. The Bowling Green, reputedly established in the late fourteenth century, still exists on the corner of Beetwell Street and South Place. Otherwise, we have only the streets with their historic names, and a handful of buildings of which the best known is surely the Peacock on Low Pavement. A large timber-framed building erected around 1500, it was originally the home of the Revell family of Carnfield Hall; it may have served as a medieval guildhall to the alderman and his council. Later an inn, it has since been officially listed and operates as the local Information and Heritage Centre.

One other relic of the medieval age remains, the most familiar of all: the church of St Mary and All Saints, with its famous crooked spire.

A medieval pottery kiln discovered during an excavation on South Street on 5 March 1999. The dig also uncovered some Roman finds.

CHAPTER 3

Aspiring: the Parish Church of St Mary and All Saints

Surely Chesterfield's most famous landmark, the parish church has come to stand as a symbol for the town itself. 'Aspire', the punning slogan beneath today's Borough Arms and the badge of the Chesterfield Borough Council, is evidence of its familiarity in Chesterfield and beyond. To most foreign visitors, if Chesterfield is famous for anything, it is as 'the town with the crooked spire'.

Christianity reached Anglo-Saxon Derbyshire in the seventh century, and it is reasonable to assume that Chesterfield had a church of some kind long before Domesday. Certainly this was the view of J.M. Bestall, and would accord with the settlement's strategic location at the midpoint of land routes moving north to south and east to west. That there was a Norman church is beyond dispute, as William Rufus in his gift to the Dean of Lincoln's newly built cathedral in 1093 specifically mentions 'the church and manor of Chesterfield.' How long this structure lasted is uncertain, but it was to be superseded by the present church building, on which work began in the thirteenth century and continued for almost 200 years. Generations of Cestrefeldians would have been born, grown old and died as craftsmen and workers laboured to raise the layers of stone higher into the sky, the building materials hauled by rope pulleys powered by huge wooden windlasses, of which the Borough Museum still holds an excellent example. Formally dedicated in 1234, St Mary and All Saints had its main

The parish church of St Mary and All Saints, displaying its famous crooked spire and the ambitious, cathedral-style cruciform design. Built over a 200-year period in the Middle Ages, the church was restored in the 1840s by Gilbert Scott. Also shown is the large churchyard, later reduced for road widening.

A builder's windlass used in the construction of Chesterfield parish church. Loads were attached to a rope wound around the axle, and the huge wheel was turned by workmen stepping inside and treading it round to raise the material to where it was needed. Left in the church tower after building was completed, it was recovered in 1947 and rebuilt in 1994. Now on display in Chesterfield Museum.

structure completed in the 1370s, and it was not until around 1400 that the tall, lead-coated spire was added to give the church its final, finishing touch.

While the town of Chesterfield was relatively small, the ecclesiastical parish it served was enormous, taking in the surrounding villages, several of which are now regarded as part of the extended borough. Newbold and Whittington to the north, Walton, Brampton and Cutthorpe to the west, Brimington, Tapton and Calow to the east and Hasland, Temple Normanton and Wingerworth to the south all came within its administrative orbit. As their 'minster church', St Mary's was of a suitably ambitious design, a massive structure built in the cruciform fashion of larger cathedral churches.

The biggest church of its kind in Derbyshire, it must have dazzled medieval worshippers, who would surely have seen nothing like it in their lives. With its 200ft spire looming over the north Derbyshire landscape and visible for miles around, St Mary's would have stood as a powerful symbol of God's might and authority over the temporal world that moved in its shadow.

Nowadays most enquirers are interested in the curiously twisted spire, and how it achieved such a strange shape. Various theories have been advanced, the most popular being the use of unseasoned wood in the original medieval construction, and subsequent buckling due to the effect of the sun's heat coupled with the weight of the lead. Bestall and others have noted that while the spire was being built the Black Death was raging through the country, and that this may have had an effect on the finished church. The bubonic plague, spread by the fleas from black rats introduced by ships returning from voyages in the Middle East, devastated entire regions, reducing England's population by anything up to one-third. Although records are mostly silent, it is hard to believe that Chesterfield remained untouched by the disease, which reached its height in 1348-49. The loss of experienced craftsmen could have led to shoddy workmanship, leaving the spire to suffer in later years. Whatever the reason, the result was a definite lean that in 1974 was found to be 8ft 6in south and 3ft 9in west.

This, though, was a problem for the future. As the Middle Ages drew to a close, Chesterfield's spire rose straight and true, a finger pointing heavenward. A mighty symbol of the spiritual life, it retained close links with the thriving merchant community surrounding it, proof of its power in a religious age. Housing the chantries of the craft, social and merchant guilds, it also served as a meeting place on its northern side which faced the old market. Nor was it untouched by the sinful nature of its parishioners, as the Foljambe butchery of their opponents in 1422 all too clearly shows. To most, however, it must have given reassurance, reminding them of the transient nature of human life, and the promise of immortality in the world beyond. Its solid stability would have seemed to echo the dawn of a new era, which saw the bloody slaughter of Lancastrians and Yorkists give way to what promised to be a more ordered time under the rule of the Tudors.

An imposing view of the church interior, from a nineteenth-century lithograph, after improvements by Victorian architect Gilbert Scott.

CHAPTER 4

Roses: the Tudors

Chesterfield entered the Tudor age as a market town whose importance rested mainly on its excellent location. At the place where all the Derbyshire trade routes met, it was a natural centre for commerce and the pursuit of wealth. The limiting factor for growth was the town's small size. It covered barely 300 acres, bounded to south and east by the rivers Hipper and Rother, barred by a series of lanes from Brampton in the west and in the north cutting off well short of present-day Stonegravels. With the exception of some common grazing land east of the Rother at Hady and Grassmoor, this tight little circle marked the limit of Chesterfield's expansion. Even more significantly, most of the 300 acres was itself taken up by waste land or the long 'burgage plots' leading from the homes and workshops of the inhabitants. The Tudor period saw the beginning of a familiar pattern, where as the population rose more and more people were packed into the same small medieval core around the church and the market-place, with the predictable results of disease and high mortality. It was a problem that would continue to plague the town well into the nineteenth century, when Chesterfield finally broke out of the encircling straitjacket of boundaries that had for so long stunted its growth.

Within this tightly limited area Chesterfield continued to operate as a successful market town, where the inhabitants still practised the ancestral trades of medieval times. Tanning, shoe-making and allied leather work were its staple industries, and with the late medieval boom in wool the production and dyeing of cloth also played an important part. There were also a few small-scale brass foundries in the town, notably that of the bell-maker Ralph Heathcote. In some cases substantial sums were made, and the acquisition of wealth enabled a number of merchants to rise in the world. This pattern had already begun in the Middle Ages, when the merchant Durant family acquired sufficient riches to build the impressive residence on Holywell Street that became known as Durant Hall. Now vanished, its site was later occupied by the old Royal Hospital, but the family name lives on in nearby Durrant Road. The old order, where the gentry held their land by blood and title, found itself obliged to admit newcomers from the world of commerce, landowners who had purchased their properties through the wealth generated by trade.

In the Middle Ages, the Walton-based Foljambes had been leading figures, and they remained a power in the Tudor age. Although some family members were implicated in the brutal murders in 1422, others were better known as high-ranking officials and public benefactors. Godfrey Foljambe, in particular, is remembered with gratitude for his endowment of Chesterfield's first grammar school, and he and his family are still honoured today in the church where the earlier killings took place. The alabaster tombs of Godfrey Foljambe and his wife Isabel may still be seen there, and are arguably the most impressive monuments of its interior. Foljambes served as High Sheriffs of Derbyshire and were major landowners under the Tudors as they had been when the Lancastrians and the Yorkists ruled. By now, though, they no longer held a monopoly on wealth and power. The merchant burgesses of Chesterfield, notably the Clarke and Heathcote families, had begun to emerge as men of importance, ready to gain their place in the sun. In 1480 their spokesmen set down in a 'composition' the written basis for a Common Council, headed by an Alderman, without seeking permission from the lord of the

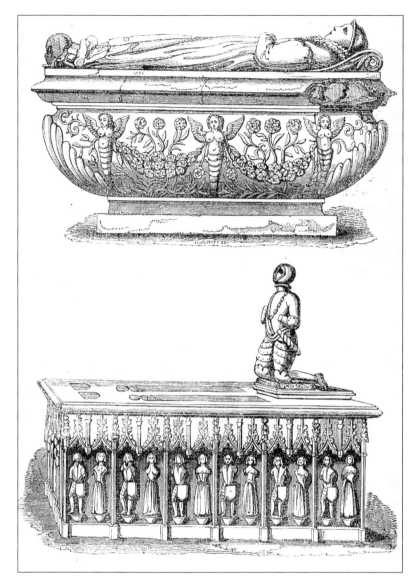

The Foljambe tombs. Perhaps the most striking monuments in the parish church, these mark the resting place of Godfrey Foljambe, a benefactor of the town, and his wife Isabel.

manor. The council gave power and a debating platform to the burgesses and their leaders. The seeds of future conflict between the 'men of Chesterfield' and the manor lord, already sown in medieval times, now bore bitter fruit.

Chesterfield's last medieval lord of the manor had been Richard Neville, Earl of Warwick. Famous as 'Warwick the Kingmaker' and a key player in the Wars of the Roses, his tenure of Chesterfield ended with his death in the battle of Barnet in 1471. It was perhaps an appropriate closing chapter to what had been a bloody age, but Neville is typical of many earlier manor lords of Chesterfield, who owned other lands and lived far away from the town, probably never setting eyes on the place. More representative of the lords of the Tudor period was George Talbot, Earl of Shrewsbury, who lived closer to hand and took a keen personal interest in how the manor was run.

Talbot, who held the lordship of Chesterfield for thirty years from 1560 to 1590, was the fourth and last husband of the ambitious Elizabeth, Countess of Shrewsbury, better known as 'Bess of Hardwick'.

The Falcon Inn, shown here in latterday guise as Everest's Falcon Dining Rooms. The Falcon dates from the sixteenth century and its structure still contains some of the original Tudor timbering.

A dynamic, strong-willed personality fitted to succeed in a male-dominated age, she became the richest woman in England by a series of dynastic marriages in which she survived all her husbands. The force behind the building of Hardwick Hall, she also involved herself in political intrigue during the reign of Elizabeth I. Her marriage to Talbot was marked by friction, and they later appear to have separated.

Talbot, who in 1568 had the onerous task of playing host to the captive Mary, Queen of Scots on behalf of his sovereign Elizabeth I, was clearly not in the best of humours during his lordship of Chesterfield, and perhaps the overbearing temper of his wife may have prompted him to assert himself over the combative burgesses from whom his bailiff collected the required rents and tolls. From the outset he dismissed their spokesmen as 'arrant knaves' and refused to admit the liberties granted them by the medieval charters.

The Middle Ages had seen the Chesterfield burgesses gradually increase their power and privileges, securing a monopoly on trades carried on in the town, with the right to examine incoming strangers, and according themselves other perquisites as 'free tenants' of the borough. These rights had been confirmed by the charters of 1204 and 1294, and having obtained them the 'men of Chesterfield' were unwilling to give them up without a fight. For his part, Talbot refused to acknowledge that his tenants had any such rights, insisting that his bailiff 'shall rule in the town as the bailiff of the lord', and battle duly commenced.

Headed by the vintner and innkeeper Ralph Clarke, the burgesses waged legal war with their lord, invoking the crown to support their ancient charters. The struggle went on for years, and a generation passed without any headway being made. Talbot remained obdurate, and was still enforcing his will on the grudging townsmen thirty years later. Indeed, for a time he appeared to have won outright, when in 1568 the burgesses were

The Free Grammar School in Victorian times. Founded from a bequest by Godfrey Foljambe in 1594, the school fell into disrepute in the Georgian era, but was rebuilt and revived in the 1840s. It produced several eminent pupils.

bullied and threatened into signing away many of their hard-won rights, including some of those guaranteed by charter, in a new document of the lord's own devising. Only in 1598, when Talbot was already eight years dead and his son Gilbert had succeeded him as manor lord, was the breakthrough made. On 20 April Queen Elizabeth in her charter of incorporation confirmed the rights given by the previous charters and granted the town its first real guaranteed measure of autonomy. It permitted the setting up of a Common Council or Corporation (the organization formed in 1480 had no real legal basis) with a mayor, six aldermen, six brethren and twelve capital burgesses, with the mayor to be elected by the aldermen. Not too surprisingly, the aldermen chose Ralph Clarke, their spokesman and leader for so many years in the battle against Talbot. The Corporation was allowed to make by-laws and enforce them on offenders by fines and imprisonment, to appoint a clerk and build a Council House. Members could own property, take legal action and make contracts, which could now be authorized by a common seal being appended to the document. Further to these provisions, the charter permitted the Corporation to build and run a grammar school, already endowed by the will of Godfrey Foljambe in 1594. In terms of self-government, Chesterfield had now arrived.

Chesterfield's industries brought wealth to the burgesses and their families, but would have done little to improve the town itself. The historian W.E. Godfrey draws a vivid and unpleasant portrait of the Tudor town, where those living in the overcrowded, insanitary rows of the Shambles would have been assailed by the combined stenches of the tanneries, the blood and filth of the butchers' slaughtering, and the clogged open channels that served as sewers running down to the Rother. These were perfect breeding conditions for disease, and in 1586 Chesterfield was hit by bubonic plague. We cannot be sure of the impact the Black Death had on the town in 1348-49, but we know that 200 years later Chesterfield suffered devastating losses. The terrifying disease raged through the town for a total of fourteen months, significantly reaching its peak in the hot June and July of 1587, claiming 54 victims in the first month and 52 in the next. From this point on the scourge of plague diminished, but by the time it finally left the town there were some 300 new graves in Chesterfield and the outlying villages. While some of these lives were lost as far east as Calow, there is little doubt that most of the victims died in Chesterfield itself, where living conditions were at their worst. Indeed, W.E. Godfrey in his article on the outbreak suspects that a handful of families may have been completely wiped out by the disease. It is difficult for the modern reader to appreciate the effect of such loss of life in a religious period when most would have regarded it as the punishment of God. It must surely have dealt a severe blow to the morale of the townsmen and their families who survived. How long it took them before Chesterfield returned to 'business as usual' is not easy to establish, but return it undoubtedly did, and by the time Queen Elizabeth confirmed the burgesses in their rights in 1598 the worst of their memories were no doubt far behind them.

Like the rest of England, Chesterfield survived the Tudor reigns without having to endure the widespread bloodshed that had marked previous ages, such as the Hundred Years War with France and the butchery of the Wars of the Roses. Henry VII and his successors offered greater stability and longer periods of peace, but their rule was not without its hazards. Henry VIII's defiance of the Papacy and the asserting of his independence began a fierce antagonism between Protestant and Catholic that endures in some places to this day. A decision taken to allow the king a second marriage and the chance to sire a male heir also led to the sacking of monastic lands and treasures, a move that made fortunes for the King and some of his more cynical followers. Even worse was the wave of religious persecution that dogged the reigns of Henry and his children, Edward, Mary and Elizabeth, as Catholic and Protestant

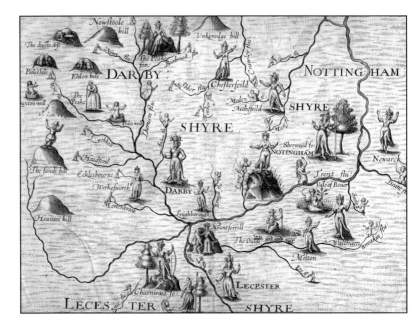

Detail from a map by William Hole, which appeared in 1622 in the 'Polyolbion', a long descriptive poem by Michael Drayton, a contemporary and drinking companion of Shakespeare. The map shows symbolic figures presiding over such landmarks as the rivers 'Ibber' (Hipper), 'Gunno' (Rother) and 'Crawley' (Doe Lea).

factions at various times gained the upper hand. Chesterfield, with a relatively small number of Catholic recusants, does not appear to have suffered unduly in this regard. On the other hand, the local guilds certainly did when their assets and property were seized in 1534 as part of the rather unpleasant 'land-grab' that marked the Dissolution of the Monasteries. This would have been a body-blow to these organizations, which must have struggled to recover.

Throughout the sixteenth century the town underwent a considerable programme of rebuilding that removed most of the old medieval houses and workshops and replaced them with more modern structures. Sadly for the health of Chesterfield, the new buildings went up on the ruins of the old, sticking closely to the same pattern of medieval streets and making them once more a haven for the plague. Like the older buildings they superseded, most of these Tudor houses have since disappeared, wiped away by a fresh wave of rebuilding in the eighteenth century. One of the more notable survivors is what was originally the Falcon Inn, which still stands on the corner of South Street and Low Pavement, close to the town centre. A large, imposing structure with the black and white half-timbering common to so many Tudor buildings and fronted by solid pillars at its entrance, much of it dates from around 1560. Later housing a café run by the Everest family and a fish restaurant, it is now occupied by the Barnsley Building Society, while the name of the inn lives on in nearby Falcon Yard. The parish church also underwent further alterations in 1500, when the row of windows known as the clerestory was added to its south transept. As the reign of Elizabeth neared its end, the men and women of Chesterfield could look back with some satisfaction, having ridden out plague, persecution and the threat of the Spanish Armada. The end of the century saw them in possession of rights and freedoms previously open to dispute, and with a corporation and elected mayor of their own. With genuine progress made, the future must have seemed bright indeed, but the years to come would bring further conflict, and once again religion would be at its heart.

CHAPTER 5

And Crowns: the Stuarts

The death of Elizabeth and the accession of her nephew James VI of Scotland to the throne marked the end of the Tudor and the beginning of the Stuart period. The people of Chesterfield probably saw no obvious change to their lives as one ruler gave way to another. Indeed, the first significant event of James's reign was the return of the dreaded plague to the town in 1608-09. This time Chesterfield suffered less badly, with eighteen burials in April followed by eight in May, but while it lasted this second unwelcome visit of the disease was no doubt just as terrifying as the first.

The new lord of the manor was William Cavendish, Earl of Newcastle. Later to be raised to a duke, this melancholy pipe-smoking grandson of Bess of Hardwick was noted for his love of horsemanship and his great wealth, and during the reign of Charles I was described as the richest man in the kingdom. Newcastle, whose residence was at Bolsover Castle some eight miles east of Chesterfield, seems to have taken a less pressing interest in the affairs of the town. While he insisted on his right to appoint a manor steward, and to oversee the manorial court, he made no real attempt to interfere with the corporation's day to day running of Chesterfield business. The charter of 1598 laid down much clearer lines of demarcation, and there are no records of the kind of disputes that marked the late Elizabethan period.

Chesterfield was finding its feet as a market town and making the most of its independence. As well as mayor and corporation, it had its own grammar school, its Council House behind Low Pavement close to the Bowling Green, and its own gaol for short-term offenders, the House of Correction built in 1614 in a damp, unwholesome location close to the river Hipper south of the town. Under the rights granted by Elizabeth's charter, it had also devised its Borough Arms for the common seal. Based on an earlier version used by the Common Council of 1480, they are found in slightly altered form in the borough's modern coat of arms. The arms used on the late Tudor seal have as their centre-piece a

A telltale plaque on the wall of Newbold Green Farm. Dated 1678, its skull and crossbones suggest that three sisters died there, probably from the frequent plagues of Tudor and Stuart times.

pomegranate tree, 'eradicated and fructed' (that is, torn out by the roots and bearing fruit) encircled by the slogan 'Sigillum Commune Burgi Cestrefeld'. Why the exotic pomegranate tree should be chosen to represent a market town in northern Derbyshire remains a mystery. Tregonwy in Cornwall and the Spanish kingdom of Granada are the only other places known to have used it as an emblem, but apparently the pomegranate signifies 'good', and perhaps the idea of fruitful growth appealed to the commercial instincts of the Chesterfield burgesses. The tree remains the central symbol of the modern coat of arms, and 'The Pomegranate' has since been adopted as the name of the former Civic Theatre on Corporation Street.

The development of commerce took further formal shape during the Stuart period with the establishing of five main trading companies in the borough. The Company of Tailors and Sadlers, the Company of Mercers, the Company of Butchers, the Company of Smiths and Braziers, and the Company of Shoemakers encompassed the range of activities carried on in Chesterfield at this time, and once more indicate how much of the town's industry still derived from its medieval origins. The Smiths and Braziers included the descendants of the bell-founder Ralph Heathcote, who were to continue the family business into the 1640s before aspiring to higher things as members of the clergy. The upward mobility of the merchant class was to be demonstrated even more dramatically by another branch of the family, descended from the Tudor butcher Thomas Heathcote but later making their mark as lead merchants. One such descendant, Gilbert Heathcote, established himself as a country gentleman at Cutthorpe Hall in the area of Brampton and Barlow west of the borough, and in later years other family members would achieve even greater success.

The world of religion had also seen radical changes. With the repression and persecution of England's Catholics, the Church of England founded by Henry VIII now found itself facing opposition from another quarter. The Tudor period had seen an increase in Puritan dissent, and in the reigns of James and his son Charles I this movement gained strength and popularity, not least in the market towns. Drawing on the austere faith of the Calvinists of Geneva, the Puritans saw themselves as chosen by God, and sought inspiration from prayer and the Bible, rather than formal ceremony. Mostly born in the age of Elizabeth when Spain was the great enemy, they decried the use of Latin in church services, seeing idolatry and 'Popery' in statues of the Virgin, and distrusting the edicts of priests and bishops. Their concept of 'stewardship' and its interpretation of the parable of the talents accorded well with a merchant lifestyle and the accumulation of wealth and profit, and Puritanism found ready converts in the business community in Chesterfield, as it did elsewhere.

The emergence of the Puritan merchant class, with their opposition to the Established Church, led to strained relations with the Crown itself. Although Charles I had followed the example of Elizabeth in 1631, confirming all previous charters and granting Chesterfield the right to hold four fairs a year, it was not long before he found himself at odds with his subjects. Finance had been a problem for James I, whose ill-fated political and military ventures drove him to desperate expedients in the raising of revenue. Charles, who inherited his father's difficulties and added a few of his own, found his authority challenged by a Parliament with a strong mercantile Puritan element, whose growing distrust of the king and his counsellors led to demands for more concessions that he was determined not to grant. 'Ship money', levied by Charles to raise funds for his decrepit navy, was one of several unpopular efforts by the king to raise the revenue he needed. At first only coastal counties were taxed, but in 1635 'Ship money' was extended inland, and Chesterfield was called upon to pay its dues. The burgesses did not take kindly to the imposition, and several made their objections plain. As time went on, and relations

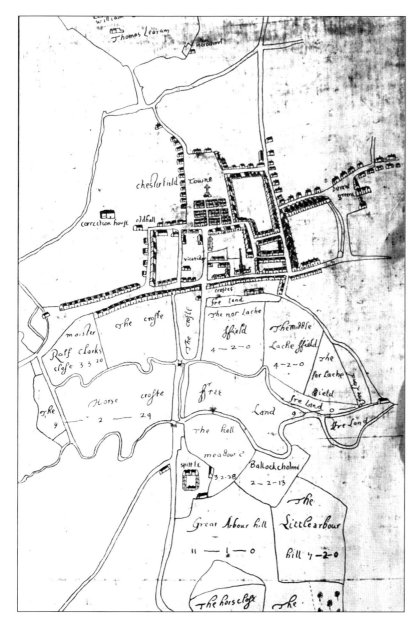

Detail from William Senior's 'Platt of Chesterfield Towne' of 1633-37, the earliest known map of the town. It reveals a small, sparsely settled area with building concentrated in the centre and an expanse of outlying plots and fields. The House of Correction, built in 1614, is situated away from the town itself.

between King and Parliament deteriorated, Chesterfield people found themselves obliged to support one side or the other. Matters were coming to a head, and the threat of civil war loomed closer.

It was at this time that the first known map of Chesterfield was drawn. The cartographer and surveyor William Senior had for several years been employed by the first and second Earls of Devonshire. Confusingly, both father and son carried the same name of William Cavendish, which was also held by their relative the Earl of Newcastle, the first Earl of Devonshire being his uncle and the second Earl his cousin. While Newcastle was lord of the manor of Chesterfield, the Earls of Devonshire owned the most land in the county, and Senior was detailed to provide a series of surveys and maps showing their properties in Derbyshire. The original survey including Chesterfield was undertaken as

early as 1610, but the map did not appear until 1637.

Entitled 'The Platt of Chesterfield Towne', Senior's map reveals a not unexpected picture of the town in the time of Charles I. It confirms our image of Chesterfield as a small, tightly cramped area of habitation concentrated around the old medieval streets, the market place and the Shambles, the remainder of the acreage taken up by plots and grazing land. The House of Correction sits some distance apart, south of the populated area close to the river; the nearest building to it is the Old Hall on the corner of Beetwell Street, opposite the Bowling Green. Senior shows the 'new' enlarged market established in the thirteenth century to the west of the grid of streets, complete with market cross. The vicarage and its extensive grounds on what is now Church Lane also appear, as does the parish church, though interestingly with no indication of a crooked spire. Whether from accuracy or diplomacy, Senior draws the spire as a straight, unwavering upward line. To the north he names Durant Green, another reminder of the successful merchant family, while to the east lie a number of crofts and fields, close to the edge of the sparse housing along today's St Mary's Gate and Lordsmill Street. One, 'Maister Ralf Clarks Close', recalls a member of the prominent burgess family involved in the legal battle with the Earl of Shrewsbury in the Tudor period. Beyond the town Senior takes in the adjoining parishes and districts, among them Brampton, Hasland, Cutthorpe, 'Spittle' (formerly the site of the leper hospital), and the unfortunately named 'Ballockholme', which would appear to correspond roughly with modern Birdholme. A study of the earlier survey confirms that the Earl of Devonshire owned several former Foljambe properties in different parts of the town, as well as plots of land outside. Of greater interest than these individual holdings, however, is the picture given us by Senior's map, the first visual image of Chesterfield in its early days of growth.

The year 1637 is unfortunately memorable for a less pleasant event. In that year thecounty assizes sat at Chesterfield, and afterwards a mass execution took place. Five men and a woman were publicly hanged at Tapton Bridge on the eastern edge of the town, a grim reminder of the law's harsh penalties at this time.

By the early 1640s, relations between King and Parliament had broken down, and the Civil War began. Charles I set up his standard at Nottingham in August 1642, and in October met an opposing army led by the Earl of Essex at Edgehill. The Royalists justifiably claimed victory in a closely fought action where they held the ground while the Parliamentarians retreated, but it was clear there would be other battles. Unlike Derby, which was solidly Parliamentarian, Chesterfield seems to have been a divided town. With Newcastle as Lord of the Manor, there must have been a fair number of Royalists, but they were not a decisive majority, and the fact that Chesterfield changed hands up to five times in the course of the war tells its own story. The town and its people were perhaps luckier than some, being bypassed by the major campaigns and battles, but their nerves must have been constantly on edge as sporadic outbreaks of fighting erupted in different parts of the county, sometimes reaching the town itself.

Sir John Gell quickly emerged as the main Parliamentary commander in the county. An ambitious, vindictive and not very likeable man, he nevertheless did more than anyone to sustain the Roundhead cause in Derbyshire for the full term of the war. Royalist leadership was assumed by William Cavendish, Earl of Newcastle, and the advantage swung from one to the other. In October 1642 Gell marched unopposed into Chesterfield and raised 200 men from the town. A year later, in November 1643, Newcastle brought his army there, having heard rumours of rebellion. He found the town already occupied by Parliamentarians under Sir Thomas Fairfax. The Royalists then 'showed themselves upon a hill within the view of the town' (probably Hady Hill which overlooks Chesterfield from the east) and fired the brush on the slope before launching their attack.

The Roundheads fled in disorder towards Nottingham, suffering casualties and leaving stragglers behind as prisoners, while Newcastle and his men reoccupied the town. It all sounds very dramatic, and no doubt it was, but judging by the small numbers involved this was more of a skirmish than a full-scale battle. There were tussles at Wingfield Manor and at Staveley Hall, where Lord Frecheville put up a stiff resistance against the besieging Roundheads, but once again these were small actions, and there seems to have been little fighting of any kind at Bolsover Castle, which surrendered to the Parliamentarians after an initial bombardment. Nothing to compare with the terrible sieges of Bristol or York, or the murderous battles in the North and Midlands that were eventually to decide the outcome of the war, these actions were typical of the minor skirmishes that marked the Civil War in most parts of the country.

It was a different story for William Cavendish, Earl of Newcastle, Chesterfield's lord of the manor. He was at the Battle of Marston Moor in 1644, where defeat cost the King control of the North to Parliament. The Earl had invested his fortune in the Royalist cause, financing his own infantry regiment, the famous 'Lambs' in their undyed woollen coats. The regiment fought to the last man at White Syke Close, and Newcastle fled to Holland, returning a ruined man at the Restoration of Charles II. In June 1645, less than a year after Marston Moor, another Roundhead win at Naseby ensured Charles's eventual defeat. The beaten king travelled through Derbyshire en route to Welbeck, halting at Lord Frecheville's home at Staveley on 20 August, but the Roundheads were not far behind, and he did not stay for long.

Compared with other counties, Derbyshire – and Chesterfield – ended the Civil War relatively undamaged, but the conflict left its scars. Apart from loved ones lost in the fighting, there would have been lost livelihoods, crops and animals stolen or left untended, homes and belongings commandeered, trade routes avoided as too dangerous to travel, and the general economic strain brought on town and county by the privations of war. The years that followed were also troubled; intrigues with the captive King by Parliament, the Army and the Scots eventually led to Charles's execution in January 1649 and the rise to power of Oliver Cromwell.

Elder Yard Unitarian chapel, Chesterfield's earliest Nonconformist place of worship, founded in 1678. This view is from the 1930s.

Friends' Meeting House on Saltergate, shown with its burial ground. George Fox visited Chesterfield in the 1650s, and the Meeting House was funded by Quaker merchant Joseph Storrs. It was demolished in the 1960s.

A gifted military leader, Cromwell the politician struggled to hold the bickering factions together, experimenting with three parliaments before taking supreme power as Lord Protector. Less intolerant than some of his colleagues, his rule was bedevilled by the rise of many Nonconformist sects often at each other's throats. While the Chesterfield burgesses were by no means all fervent Royalists, they probably stopped short of the more extreme Puritan sects and their beliefs. The Commonwealth government crushed rebellion at home and proved its strength abroad, but bans on May Day celebrations and horse-racing were resented, as were the heavy taxes.

When the rule of the major-generals was imposed in 1655, the people grew increasingly discontented, and when Cromwell died three years later most were ready for a change. The most interesting local development of these troubled times was the compilation of the Scarsdale surveys. Begun in 1652 by the Parliamentary commissioners, these assessed the agricultural and industrial state of the Scarsdale Hundred, parish by parish, and were continued into the first years of Charles II's reign. The surveys are especially interesting for the picture they give of Chesterfield in relation to the parishes around, a picture already hinted at by Senior's map of 1637. Scarsdale emerges as one of the most important areas of Derbyshire, both for agriculture and the growth of industries. Chesterfield, on the other hand, while still the main market town of the region and the focus for Scarsdale's farmers, clearly lags behind its neighbours in terms of 'heavy industry'. Coal and ironstone mines, forges and charcoal-fired blast furnaces were appearing in substantial numbers in most of the outlying parishes. To the north-east, Staveley had a forge and furnace in addition to its two corn mills, while further off in Renishaw and Eckington the Sitwell family had established what was to become a major ironworks. To the west and south-west was a greater concentration of new industries, with Walton boasting three smelting houses and a lead mill, Brampton four smelting houses, and Wingerworth a forge and furnace. In coming years the landowners who had encouraged these developments – at

Wingerworth the Hunlokes, at Staveley the Frechevilles, and in Eckington and Renishaw the Sitwells – would benefit from their new industries in a way that Chesterfield was unable to match. The concentration of smelting houses in Brampton is also significant, as within 200 years that parish would experience a phenomenal industrial growth that in time would make it an attractive prize for its larger urban neighbour.

In marked contrast to the industrial development outside its boundaries, Chesterfield continued to operate through its market, its position midway along the major trade routes in the county, and its traditional small-scale industries. While agriculture stayed the main occupation, such a position was sustainable. But as industries grew all around in the eighteenth and early nineteenth centuries, Chesterfield would find itself isolated and something of a backwater as its own declining trades stagnated.

The emergence of the Nonconformists led to the founding of various dissenting congregations in the town. One of the earliest was the Society of Friends, better known as the Quakers. In the 1650s Chesterfield was visited by George Fox, the founder of the movement, and his lieutenant James Naylor. The Quakers were frequently in trouble with the authorities for their outspoken public criticism of the government and for such habits as their refusal to remove their hats to anyone but God Himself, and Fox spent a night in the House of Correction before going on to Derby.

The Dissenters had gained a firm footing in the town by the time Charles II was restored to the throne in 1660. His return, marked by public rejoicing in Derbyshire, may have been less welcome to Chesterfield's civic leaders. Some of these were no doubt political appointments, holding office as a result of their Roundhead sympathies, but they probably represented a substantial body of feeling in a town where the mercantile Puritan ethic was strong. The new king, a more wily politician than his father, and determined not to 'go on his travels' again, made sure Parliament was dominated by his own supporters, and ready to pass laws to enforce obedience. He was suspicious of the towns with their dissenting communities, in his view potential hotbeds of sedition.

The Corporation Act of 1661 passed by the 'Cavalier' Parliament enforced an oath of loyalty on anyone holding public office, while the Anglican ceremony and the Book of Common Prayer returned to every church. Chesterfield's town fathers came under immediate pressure, and several were ejected from office. Mayor Hercules Clay refused to take the loyalty oath and was removed, four of his aldermen going with him, while at St Mary's the Presbyterian vicar also departed. Both men were replaced by those with views more acceptable to the crown. The corporation and the town survived the blow, and once the changes had been made Chesterfield continued much as before. One minor but interesting decision made by the burgesses came in 1671 when Richard Clarke, vintner and former mayor, convinced his fellows to melt down the corporation plate and make an official mace. The borough arms were then emblazoned on a shield on the mace itself.

By this time a ceremony had been perfected for the annual mayor-making, where the mayor was proclaimed at the market cross and in the main streets, the festivities also including a sermon and afterwards the mayor's feast. Whatever else was happening, the town fathers evidently knew how to enjoy themselves!

With Charles II on the throne the country returned to some kind of stability, and the avoidance of any major domestic strife. All the same, the King spent most of his reign walking a political tightrope, maintaining the power of the crown and the established church while concealing his own unpopular Catholic sympathies. An astute politician, Charles managed the difficult balancing act and died as king of a peaceful realm, but the old divisions and discontents were bubbling away beneath the surface. They were to burst violently into the open after his death, in a new rebellion which would once more unseat a Stuart king from his throne.

CHAPTER 6

Cock and Pynot:
the Glorious Revolution of 1688

James, Duke of York, who succeeded Charles to the throne as James II in 1685, was an altogether different personality from his elder brother. A talented soldier who served in the French and Spanish armies under Conde and Turenne, he was strong-willed and outspoken, and from the beginning made no secret of his Catholic beliefs, which he was more than ready to force on an unwilling nation. This, in a land where for almost two centuries Catholics were regarded as natural enemies, was a recipe for disaster. In our more enlightened times this virulent hatred of Roman Catholics seems unnatural and unpleasant, but in the 1680s and for long afterwards, it was very real. To the Elizabethans, Catholics were the allies of Spain, the arch-enemy who came close to destroying them. To the Puritans of the 1640s and 1650s, they were agents of the Devil, spreading 'Popery' like a lethal plague. Once James's own Catholicism became known, unease took hold on the minds of most of his subjects. For the first time since Mary Tudor, England had a Roman Catholic monarch. What was to prevent him enforcing his religion on everyone? Would it mean a return to the Inquisition, the bonfires of Protestant martyrs, as it had done in Mary's reign? Such questions, however ridiculous they may now seem, were being asked in homes across the country in the 1680s.

Nor, indeed, were they so ridiculous. James's first move was to set aside the Test Act, which prevented Catholics from holding public office. He did so in defiance of the Parliament, which refused to repeal the act. He also tried, unsuccessfully, to abolish Habeas Corpus, which would have allowed him to make arbitrary arrests anywhere in the country. James made sure all military and naval senior officers were personal appointments, and began to install his favourites in positions of power. His close

Revolution House, Old Whittington. As the Cock and Pynot inn, it was the meeting place for the Earl of Devonshire and his fellow plotters in 1688. Purchased by Chesterfield Borough Council, it is now preserved as a tourist attraction.

ties with Louis XIV of France, in whose army he had served, were another cause for concern, and he made matters worse by receiving funds from his old master. The stage was set for rebellion, and it was not long in coming.

It flared quickly in the west, only to be brutally stamped out. James, Duke of Monmouth, the illegitimate son of Charles II, landed at Lyme Regis on 11 June 1685 and by the following month had raised 6,000 men, but from the beginning his venture was doomed. King James infiltrated his London organization, an uprising in Scotland fizzled out, and when Monmouth's army was finally brought to battle at Sedgemoor on 6 July, his raw volunteers were cut to pieces by hard-bitten regulars under the effective command of Sir John Churchill, later Duke of Marlborough. The survivors came to trial before the merciless Judge Jeffreys, who at his 'Bloody Assizes' sentenced some 300 to the gallows. Monmouth, pleading for his life, was shown no mercy and singled out for a gruesome execution. Hundreds of rebels were shipped as slaves to West Indian sugar plantations, while Dorset and Somerset were subjected to a reign of terror. James had shown what his enemies could expect if they ventured to defy him.

The failure of Monmouth's rebellion did nothing to quell the nation's discontent with its king. His harsh, intolerant rule angered many, and resentment continued to smoulder. James thought himself safe, but opposition had merely been driven underground. Unable to defy their king openly, his enemies plotted to have him replaced.

Their choice was the Dutch prince William of Orange, the husband of James's daughter Mary and thus preserving a link with the House of Stuart. Unlike James, William was a staunch Protestant, and could be relied upon to guarantee the Protestant religion in England should he gain the throne. And it was to be in Derbyshire that events were set in motion to bring it about.

Some time prior to June 1688 three Derbyshire gentlemen met on horseback on Whittington Moor to the north of Chesterfield. The moor by this time served as a venue for horse-racing and hunting, which gave a plausible excuse for their meeting. The three were William Cavendish, Earl of Devonshire, the Earl of Danby, and Mr John D'Arcy, and they met to plan the invitation of William of Orange to come over and seize the throne. Devonshire, an intriguing personality, was a notorious womanizer, a fighter of duels, and the writer of undistinguished poetic effusions. A well-known figure at court, he had fallen foul of James after two bouts of fisticuffs outside the royal apartments where he got the better of the king's supporter Col. Culpeper, and after the second encounter was fined and briefly imprisoned. The largest landowner in Derbyshire, he saw his position as being under threat from the king's favourites, and the fact that he was a prominent conspirator shows the strength of feeling against

William Cavendish, 4th Earl and 1st Duke of Devonshire. A quarrelsome, fearless and charismatic personality, he played a leading role in the 'Glorious Revolution' of 1688 that drove James II from his throne. Rewarded with a Dukedom by a grateful William III, he was hailed as 'the patron of our liberty'. (Devonshire Collection, Chatsworth. Reproduced by permission of the Duke of Devonshire and the Chatsworth Settlement Trustees. Photograph: Photographic Survey, Courtauld Institute of Art.)

The later version of Chesterfield Borough Arms, currently in use. The central emblem of the pomegranate tree is now supported by the figures of cock and pynot (magpie) both wearing ducal crowns, a reference to the Duke of Devonshire's plotting at the Cock and Pynot inn, now the Revolution House. The figure on the crest is the Derby ram, while the motto refers in punning fashion to the crooked spire.

James and his policies. A shower of rain coming on, the conspirators left the moor and moved to the nearby village of Old Whittington, where they continued their discussion in the parlour of the Cock and Pynot (magpie) inn. Devonshire and his fellow plotters signed the invitation, which was to be sent in coded form to William at the Hague. Their discussion over, they went their separate ways, Danby agreeing to raise rebellion in the North while Devonshire took responsibility for the Midlands. It is as well to remember just how dangerous an enterprise this was in 1688. Whatever their reasons, these men were taking a fearful risk, and Monmouth's fate reminded them of what would happen if they failed.

Shortly afterwards William of Orange received the invitation to come over and rule as king of England. James, aware of the coming invasion, counted on his ally the King of France to keep William busy, but Louis decided to attack Germany rather than Holland, and William seized his chance. When he landed at Torbay on 5 November 1688, the expected resistance never materialized, and William found himself at the head of the first successful invasion of England since his namesake William the Conqueror. But this time the invaders proved far more welcome.

Devonshire had done his bit, reading a 'Declaration in Defence of the Protestant Religion' to an assembled crowd in Derby before dashing off to Nottingham and raising a cavalry regiment. Ready as ever for a fight, he discovered the war was over. Princess Anne joined him at Nottingham, while the King, preparing for battle, suddenly found he had run out of friends. Most damaging of all was the desertion of Sir John Churchill, who at this crucial stage decided to stand aside.

A card advertising the Chesterfield Races of 1758. Founded by the Duke of Devonshire, always a leading patron, in the time of Charles II, the races were a popular attraction for almost 300 years. Entrants shown here include Lord Byron and the Marquis of Rockingham. The last races were run in July 1924.

A

LIST of the HORSES, &c.

Entered to RUN

On Chesterfield Course, 1758.

Chesterfield Races. A large crowd and several motor vehicles are in evidence in the 1920s. The event was extremely popular, drawing crowds of up to 50,000 in the early part of the twentieth century.

Chesterfield Races. A jockey in combative pose, probably celebrating a win, at a meeting in the early 1920s.

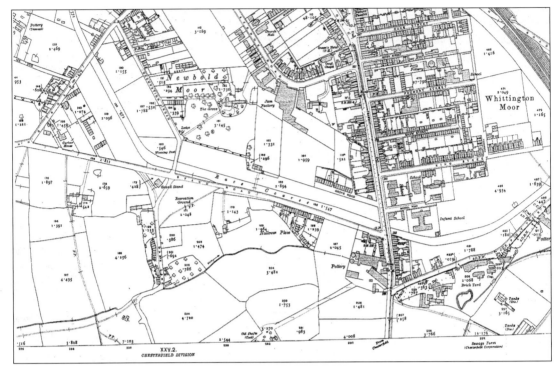

Detail from an Ordnance Survey map of 1916, showing the two-mile layout of the racecourse at Whittington Moor. The races continued until July 1924, and are still recalled today by names like Racecourse Road and Stand Road.

Unable to risk a battle, England's last Catholic king fled without a fight from the country he had previously ruled with an iron hand. Two years later, in Ireland, he and William met again at the Battle of the Boyne, where James was finally defeated and William's rule confirmed.

The departure of the hated James was marked by rejoicing as great as that which had greeted his brother's Restoration. Given the ease with which he had been overthrown, it is hardly surprising that his liberated subjects hailed the 'Glorious' or 'Bloodless Revolution' as a triumph of freedom, justice and the Protestant faith. Where Monmouth's rebellion had been a muddled, bloody failure the revolution of 1688 achieved total success with hardly a blow being struck. Nowhere was celebration greater than in Whittington, where the plotters of the 'Cock and Pynot' were regarded as heroes, the Earl of Devonshire especially being lauded as 'the patron of our liberty'.

Viewed from our later perspective, it is hard for us to grasp the importance of the Glorious Revolution for those alive at the time. To the modern reader, the meeting at the 'Cock and Pynot' and James's eventual downfall are something that happened in history, and now long past. In fact the 1688 Revolution was a defining moment not only in English history, but in the way English people came to see themselves. Even under Elizabeth's rule, there had always been the danger of a Catholic victory and the suppression of the Protestant faith. Now, with William's arrival and the flight of James, England's future as a Protestant country was guaranteed, and the English were free to assert their true identity as a Protestant nation. The slogan of 'a free Parliament and a Protestant religion' neatly summed up the

views of most Englishmen of the time. This attitude, and the tendency to regard Catholics as potentially dangerous outsiders, was effectively authorized by the triumph of 1688. It was to continue with very little alteration through the eighteenth and nineteenth centuries, and in parts of Ireland it unfortunately continues to this day.

The Derbyshire gentry's key role in the uprising was recognized. Devonshire, the leading plotter, duly received the lion's share of rewards. Created first Duke of Devonshire, Lord Lieutenant of Derbyshire and Lord High Steward of England (he carried the crown on ceremonial occasions), he was also granted Crown Rights to the High Peak Hundred, and profited from the lucrative lead mines around Castleton. His part in the conspiracy saw him raised to even greater wealth and power as a close confidant of the new king. At a local level, the choice of Whittington as the venue for his plottings further emphasizes the association of the Dukes of Devonshire with the Chesterfield Races at Whittington Moor, and with the town of Chesterfield itself.

As for Whittington, the village where the historic meeting had taken place, it too entered the realm of local folklore. The old Cock and Pynot was afterwards preserved as the Revolution House; a historic monument in its own right, it was purchased by the Chesterfield Corporation in 1938, and is now kept as a museum. The figures of the Cock and Pynot (Magpie) are nowadays used as supporters to the borough coat of arms, further incorporating the event into Chesterfield's history. Enthusiasm remained as strong 100 years after the event, when in 1788 massive celebrations were held in Derbyshire and throughout the country to mark the centenary of the Revolution; 200 years later, well into Victorian times, it was still slow to die.

The Glorious Revolution established the self-image of the English as a Protestant nation whose prosperity was based on commerce. It was an image that accorded well with the burgesses of the market town of Chesterfield, and one to which they attempted to conform as the seventeenth century drew to a close and the reign of the later Stuarts gave way to that of the Hanoverian kings.

CHAPTER 7

Urban Decay, Suburban Elegance:
Chesterfield in the Georgian Age

The eighteenth and early nineteeth centuries saw England ruled by four German kings, all bearing the name of George. The first of these spoke only German, as did his son and successor, but the line gradually acquired an English character in the reign of George III, who spoke the language and asserted 'I glory in the name of Britain!' What counted for most of their subjects was that they were Protestants, and that under their rule the Protestant faith would continue to be upheld.

After the scares of the 1715 and 1745 rebellions, the country settled down to what is now remembered as an age of elegance, of beautiful buildings and gardens, great literature from Pope, Dryden, Scott and Jane Austen, and the music of Handel and Haydn. Like most pictures of this kind, it had a darker side, the elegance underlain by filth, poverty and disease. Chesterfield, in common with everywhere else, had something of both. As the eighteenth century approached, Chesterfield showed little change from the place it had been in Tudor and Stuart times. Just as before, its main importance was as a centre for the marketing of lead, corn, farm produce and the goods made by its own tradesmen. The large market place was its main feature, and continued to take the eye of most visitors. This was how the town looked to Celia Fiennes on her visit in 1697:

'Chesterfield looks low when you approach it from the adjacent hill which you descend, but then you ascend another to it; the Coale pitts and quaraes of stone are all about even just at the town end, and in the town its all built of stone; the Church stands in a place of eminency, the town looks well, the Streets good the Market very large; it was Satturday which is their market day and there was a great Market like some little faire, a great deale of corne and all sorts of ware

Market Place, looking towards High Street, c. 1800. Still a thriving market town in Georgian times, Chesterfield had begun to suffer from urban decay that would have to be tackled at the end of the century.

and fowles, there I bought my self 2 very good fatt white (pullings as they call them) pullets for 6 pence both, and I am sure they were as large and as good as would have cost 18 pence if not two shillings apiece in London, so said all my Company; in this town is the best ale in the kingdom generally esteem'd.'

Once again the contrast is brought home, of industrialization (the 'Coale pitts and quaraes') in full swing only yards outside the borough ('at the town end'), while inside Chesterfield itself the main attraction is the market and its bargains. Rather more disconcertingly, Daniel Defoe appears to have found the town virtually unchanged nearly thirty years later. 'Chesterfield,' the author of *Robinson Crusoe* and *Moll Flanders* informs us, 'is a handsome populous town, well-built and well inhabited, notwithstanding it stands in the farthest part of this rocky country; for being on the north west side next to Yorkshire, it enters Scarsdale, which is a rich fruitful part of the country, though surrounded with barren moors and mountains…Here is, however, nothing remarkable in this town but a free school, and a very good market, well stored with provisions; for here is little or no manufacture.'

Chesterfield, in 1724 as in 1697, clung to its old craft industries, whose trading companies had now taken over the restrictive, protectionist attitudes of the medieval guilds. Strangers entering the town in order to trade were liable to fines, as were the landlords who put them up for the night. In fact, the first division of Chesterfield into administrative wards was to make it easier for the local aldermen to track down strangers and prevent them living there! With the town dominated by this kind of outlook, and its affairs run by a small group of merchant families, Chesterfield became increasingly isolated from the developments beyond its boundaries. The roads that led into the town were its lifeblood, and it still served as a focal point for the passage and trade of goods, but inside the boundaries stagnation had already begun, with the old medieval centre packed to bursting, and many buildings showing signs of decay. It was a position that could not be sustained indefinitely if Chesterfield was to grow and prosper in future.

Celia Fiennes's comment on the town having 'the best ale in the kingdom' is also worth noting. By the 1740s Chesterfield boasted four malthouses, the beginning of an industry that would provide rich returns to the town fathers in later centuries. Predictably, though, these were outnumbered by no less than nine tanneries, showing that the leather trade still had a stranglehold inside the borough. Tanneries and malthouses alike were concentrated at the south end of town, Low Pavement and Lordsmill Street accommodating most, while a large number of butchers still plied their trade in the Shambles. More housing was now crowded into the dark, narrow yards, and the noise and stench can only be imagined. If anything, central Chesterfield with its close-packed population, open sewers and cramped, derelict buildings would have been more noisome, foul and disease-ridden in the Georgian age than it had been in Tudor times.

There were some improvements, and the eighteenth century saw the appearance of several social amenities. The parish workhouse was set up on South Place in the 1730s and, although actuated by mainly economic motives (better to have the poor work for their keep than to be recipients of poor relief), it served a useful purpose. Two sets of almshouses were built, in 1703 and 1751. John Carr's town hall, its construction financed by the Duke of Portland (now Lord of the Manor) became an admired feature at the north side of the market place by 1788, where it was used by the manorial court and the county magistrates, and Chesterfield's first corporation theatre was established in Theatre Yard, off Low Pavement. A new building for the Free Grammar School was erected in 1710, and turned out many eminent pupils. The most famous alumnus of the earlier grammar school had been Thomas Secker, who later became Archbishop of Canterbury and whose house may still be seen at the corner of New Square. This house, together with the terrace on Saltergate, must rank as Chesterfield's finest examples of Georgian architecture.

Nevertheless, it was beyond the town that the rate of change was greatest. The roads that homed in on Chesterfield, bearing the heavy carts with their cargoes of lead, millstones and grain, had begun to take severe punishment from the volume of traffic, and a major overhaul was needed. The mid-eighteenth century saw the setting up of turnpike roads under the control of local turnpike trusts. These roads, maintained by tolls levied on their users, were a marked improvement on their predecessors. The Bakewell-Chesterfield and Worksop turnpike was approved in 1739, and was quickly followed by further routes from Derby and Matlock. Even so, road transport remained slow and expensive, and many manufacturers preferred to move their goods by water when this was possible. The Chesterfield Canal, officially opened in 1777, was a pioneering step forward, offering the chance of a quicker and cheaper supply of goods to the buyer. The brainchild of the great engineer James Brindley, it ran 46 miles from Chesterfield to Stockwith near Gainsborough in Lincolnshire, and was built at a cost of £160,000. Once in operation, it rewarded its shareholders, running at a fair profit for almost half a century. Sadly, Brindley did not live to see his canal open, dying in 1772 shortly after the Act was passed in Parliament.

Chesterfield's burgesses, who had looked askance on the turnpike roads, showed a fair amount of opposition to the canal, which was seen as a threat to their trade. This attitude, though, was not unanimous, and several leading property-owners in the town involved themselves in the canal at an early stage. Men like the merchants Samuel Jebb and Isaac Wilkinson, mine-owner John Frith, Godfrey Heathcote and the attorney Anthony Lax were quick to see the opportunities offered by this new mode of transport, and bought shares in the organization. These men, and others, played key roles in the Canal Company during its formative period, and profited as a result. While their actions stemmed from self-interest, they were more far-sighted than their fellows, and showed an awareness of new developments that was sadly lacking in the corporation as a whole.

The town continued to turn out men of enterprise, but itself showed few signs of real progress. All but bypassed by the Industrial Revolution now booming in the surrounding parishes, it clung to cottage-style industries such as the hosiery manufacture which thrived in the 1780s but which disappeared within fifty years. The town's first factory, Tucker's Silk Mill on the corner of Beetwell Street, began operations in 1786, having probably served as a cutlery factory shortly before. Like all Chesterfield's industries, it was overshadowed by the complex of furnaces, forges and mills founded in Brampton ten years earlier by John Smith and carried on by his grandson Ebenezer as the Griffin Foundry, a business that in the Napoleonic wars employed 1,200 workers. This massive enterprise, operating within sight of the borough, was enough to put the town fathers to shame. As it expanded, the Smiths threatened to encircle the borough, with their Adelphi ironworks at Duckmanton, coal mines at Staveley and Boythorpe, and ironstone workings in Ashgate, Brampton, Walton, Wingerworth and Hady.

Another development of a more recreational kind was the racecourse at Whittington Moor, where William Cavendish and his fellow conspirators had met in 1688. Races had been run there from the time of Charles II, the Earl of Devonshire being the original founder of the enterprise. By the eighteenth century the 'Chesterfield Races' had become a regular annual event with a large attendance from far beyond Chesterfield itself. The course, which extended for two miles and crossed the main

WALTON LODGE,
Family Mansion & Estate,
DERBYSHIRE.

8 Miles from *Matlock*, and 24 from *Buxton*.

To be Sold,
(BY PRIVATE CONTRACT)
ALL THAT VERY DESIRABLE

FREEHOLD
MANSION AND ESTATE,

MOST ELIGIBLY-SITUATED AT WALTON, IN THE PARISH OF CHESTERFIELD,
IN THE SAID COUNTY OF DERBY,
CONTAINING (BY SURVEY)

129*A.* 1*R.* 37*P.* of Land,

As hereinafter particularly described.

THE MANSION HOUSE (though not at all placed upon a high, or in an exposed situation) commands most extensive prospects over a beautiful and varied part of the *Hundred of Scarsdale*, which is most richly Wooded &c.—THE LAND around the Mansion, lies all within a Ring-Fence, is in good condition, and adjoins the Turnpike Road between CHESTERFIELD and MATLOCK—from the former of which places (the Post town) the Estate is only 3 Miles—and from the latter 8 Miles.

THE MANSION HOUSE has been built only about Twenty Years, and consists of a handsome Vestibule (or front Hall) and Portico—together with a Back-Hall and Staircase—also an excellent Dining, Drawing, and Breakfast Room, upon the Ground-floor, (exclusive of Offices of every description) with Seven good family Bed Chambers, (exclusive of Servants' ditto) over the same.—There is also good Stabling for Ten Horses, Two Coach-houses, Barn, Cow-houses, Fold, Yard, and all other requisite Out-Offices.—Together with a Walled-in Kitchen Garden, Fish-Ponds, Cold Bath &c—The Shrubberies and Plantations, in different parts of the Estate, are in a most thriving condition, and there is a valuable Spring-Wood, of about Three Acres, very full of Timber, and Reserves.——*The Whole, forming a most desirable Residence for a Gentleman's Family.*

Details of the sale of Walton Lodge and estate in 1820. This eminently desirable Georgian residence was the home of the merchant Samuel Jebb in the eighteenth century.

Sheffield-Chesterfield road at four points, is now marked only by streets with the telltale names of Racecourse Road and Stand Road. Attended by the Duke of Devonshire and the aristocracy, it also attracted a criminal element that made it an unwelcome venue to some respectable tradesmen and their families. It was popular with most Chesterfield people, however, and it became a custom for the church bells to be rung when the races were run, a practice discontinued by the disapproving vicar in 1829. This did nothing to dispel the widespread support for the races, which continued into the twentieth century, only coming to an end in July 1924. St Mary's church, it seems, was in greater need of help than Chesterfield Races. In common with other buildings in the town it was showing its age, and underwent an almost continuous series of roof repairs between 1769 and 1774. The spire was a particular cause for concern, as by now there was no hiding its obvious leaning askew from the rest of the building. Efforts were made to patch it up in 1784, but by 1817 a survey recommended that the famous spire should be demolished in the interests of safety. The view was not accepted by the church authorities, and in 1819 yet more repairs were made. None made any difference to the 'crooked spire', which now spawned a variety of stories as to how it came about. Ranging from the spire bowing in admiration to a beautiful young bride to the Devil catching his tail around it, these legends have now

*Two modern views of
Walton Lodge, now the
home of Mr Peter
Sutherland.*

entered the realm of local folklore. It was in the early nineteeth century, too, that an anonymous versifier penned the well-known lines:

'Whichever way you turn your eye

It always seems to be awry.'

By this time the parish church had definite competition from other places of worship in the town. The nonconformist sects, persecuted under Charles I and at the Restoration, had returned in greater strength on the surge of patriotic Protestantism that had marked the Glorious Revolution, and made their presence felt in Chesterfield before the end of the seventeenth century. The Elder Yard chapel was founded in 1694 on a site purchased by the former Parliamentarian sympathizer Cornelius Clarke. Jointly used for a time by those old enemies the Presbyterians and the Independents, it had become a Unitarian chapel by 1818. The Independents (better known as the Congregationalists) broke away late in the eighteenth century, eventually setting up the Rose Hill Independent chapel in 1822.

Elder Yard was quickly followed by the Meeting House of the Society of Friends, the Quakers, on Saltergate, which opened in 1697. George Fox had made willing disciples in the town, whose number included businessmen like John Frith and William Storrs, another lead merchant. Belief and business went hand in hand for the Quakers, who were keen adherents of the old Puritan doctrine of 'stewardship' and making use of God-given talents. William Storrs, the merchant, was responsible for the building of the Meeting House. Another major denomination, the Baptists, built their chapel in 1817. Most dramatic of these new arrivals were the Methodists, whose emergence as a religious body dominated the eighteenth and early nineteenth centuries. In 1776, a hundred years after Fox's visit to Chesterfield and his sojourn in the House of Correction, John Wesley rode into the town and preached a rousing sermon from the steps on the north side of the Market Place, returning to repeat the experience a year later. By 1795 Chesterfield had its first Methodist meeting-place, the Wesleyan chapel on Saltergate, and a short time later the Wesleyan Circuit was established in the town. The later, more radical hellfire approach of the Primitive Methodists was slower to catch on in Chesterfield; the movement had founded chapels at Brampton and Whittington in the 1820s, but Chesterfield's 'Prims' chapel did not appear until 1848. Appealing to the working man, and often seeking congregations where the Anglican church had no regular presence, the Methodists were the religious success story of the Georgian period, and quickly became the main Nonconformist group in the town.

The first years of the nineteenth century brought other visitors to Chesterfield. In 1803 the town provided accommodation for French prisoners of war captured by British forces and currently on parole. These new guests of the town were mostly army and naval officers, including several of senior rank, and their servants. While the majority were French

Tapton Grove. Built by Avery Jebb, brother of Samuel, in the 1790s, this elegant Georgian house is typical of suburban residences located outside the overcrowded, unhealthy borough of Chesterfield. It was also close to Tapton House, later the home of George Stephenson.

Canal bridge at Lockoford Lane, following reconstruction in 1931, with the original date of 1777 incised in the arch. Designed by James Brindley, the Chesterfield Canal ran from Wharf Lane in the town to Stockwith, near Gainsborough, and was the main transport route for goods prior to the advent of the railways.

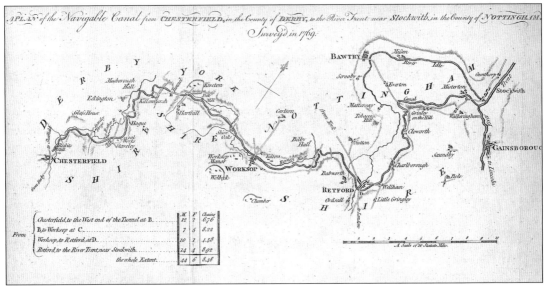

Map of the proposed Chesterfield Canal in 1771. Opened in 1777 at a cost of £165,000, the canal ran 45 miles from Chesterfield to Stockwith. It had 65 locks and 2 tunnels, of which the 3,000-yard Norwood Tunnel was the longest in the country when opened.

nationals, the listing of names shows a number of Poles and the entry for the servant of General Charles D'Henin reads 'Paul (Black)'. As General D'Henin had served in the Caribbean, it seems likely that Paul was a French Caribbean citizen. Many of the prisoners had recently served in the campaign to recapture the island of Haiti from the former slave army commanded by Toussaint L'Ouverture, where Napoleon had shown an unpleasant racist streak in his determination to crush the rebels by the most brutal methods.

In the end, Haiti had become a Vietnam-style situation for the French, as military reverses and yellow fever forced them to withdraw. The French officers in Chesterfield were disgusted by the cruelty of some of their leaders, and General Rochambeau, notorious for his brutality in Haiti, was shunned by the other prisoners. He and General Boyer were removed to other towns to avoid further trouble. General D'Henin was far more popular with Chesterfield people, and while in the town married a Scottish lady who was living there. After his release the couple returned to Paris, but the General's luck ran out when he served at Waterloo, a cannon shot taking off his leg.

The town did its best to make its new guests feel at home, and the uniformed officers became a familiar sight taking their daily promenade along High Street and Middle Pavement. Chesterfield having no Roman Catholic church of its own, Sir Henry Hunloke – himself a Catholic – offered the prisoners the use of his private chapel at Wingerworth for their devotions. The story goes that, in order to get around the rule that the prisoners must not travel more than a mile from the town, Hunloke had the Wingerworth milestone removed and carried to the chapel in front of the prisoners! It makes an appealing, if unsubstantiated, story.

Friendships were made with the people of the town, and several officers married Chesterfield ladies. One man, a Pole, stayed behind when the others left and earned his living as a farmer. His name is given as 'Preski' and he is described 'the servant of an officer of high rank.' No Preski appears in the list of French prisoners, but 'Preski' may have been 'Jean Brcsky, servant to Col. Philip de Gaetze' who is one of the entries there. With a name so difficult to pronounce, Brcsky seems a likely candidate for the man who became 'Preski', and there are certainly several families with the surname Preskey in the north-east of Derbyshire.

Some did not wait to be released. Aided by Jonas Lawton, a local surgeon's assistant, General Excelmans and Col. De la Grange escaped from the town in a covered cart and made their way to Paris. Like D'Henin, Excelmans made the mistake of rejoining his Emperor at Waterloo, and later served twenty years in prison. Lawton's error was to come back and try again. His second attempt at a rescue came to grief, and he and the escaping French prisoner were captured, Lawton serving two years in Derby gaol.

Another escapee was Col. Richemont, who behaved in a rather ungentlemanly fashion. He fled Chesterfield leaving a number of unpaid debts which were never recovered. Ironically, Richemont was the victim of a dramatic incident described in the *Star* newspaper of 1807, when £1,000 was stolen from his strong-box while he was lodging at the Falcon inn. A search revealed the thief to be a fellow prisoner, who admitted his guilt and promptly swallowed poison; not content with this, the wretched man seized a knife and stabbed himself in the breast. A coroner's jury returned a verdict of 'self-murder' on the unnamed man, who was laid to rest where four roads crossed, and a stake driven into his side. Evidently fear of vampires was still strong in Chesterfield in the early nineteenth century.

Fortunately, these were rare cases, and most of the prisoners behaved well during their stay. They also provided gifts of their own. Several proved excellent craftsmen, carving intricate models from bone and ivory, a speciality being model men-of-war ships, and also introduced a particular style of glove-making to the town which used a bone crook for a crocheted effect and was later adopted by Chesterfield's ladies. When they left in 1814, many Chesterfield people were sad to see them go.

The early nineteenth century saw a significant increase in the town's population, which grew by roughly one-third in the period 1801-1831. This merely served to emphasize the overcrowding, and the need for basic improvements, and these years were also marked by the appearance of piped water and gas lighting, both introduced in the 1820s. With the replacement of open drains by closed sewers in the 1830s, these must have been welcome developments for the people living in the cramped 300 acres of the borough. On the educational front, a national school was founded in 1814, and an infant school in

1829, and these were matched by a number of financial institutions. A savings bank operated from 12 to 1 p.m. every Monday in 1816, and the Chesterfield and North Derbyshire Banking Company opened its doors full-time in 1834, while a Benevolent Society was formed in 1826.

The town was by now beginning to take a look at itself. Its first history, the Revd George Hall's *History of Chesterfield*, appeared as a slim volume in 1823. It was followed not long afterwards by what is known to most as 'Ford's History', as it was produced and sold by local bookseller Thomas Ford from his premises in Irongate. A more weighty tome, this work admits no author, using Hall's original text and making substantial additions of its own. Lively and anecdotal in style, the text is enlivened by several engravings and takes in not only Chesterfield but other Derbyshire places of interest. While its accuracy has often been called into question by later, more scholarly historians, Ford provides the modern reader with an entertaining view of his town as it appeared to its Georgian inhabitants.

Old Silk Mill, South Place. Believed to be Chesterfield's first factory, this was a residence in 1750, and probably served as a cutlery factory before being used for silk manufacture in the 1780s. It is shown prior to demolition in the 1960s.

Standing at the junction of Beetwell Street and South Place, Beetwell Old Hall was one of Chesterfield's oldest buildings. It appears to have been the home of Joshua Jebb in the eighteenth century. The hall has since been demolished.

While Ford and Hall took care of Chesterfield's past, its present and future came under scrutiny from the Roberts family, who gave the town its first home-produced newspaper when the *Chesterfield Gazette* made its debut appearance in 1828. Later to be better known as the *Derbyshire Courier*, the paper kept its readers up to date with national and international news as well as 'local intelligence' and a wealth of advertisements ranging from miracle cures to the sale of agricultural implements. It was still dispensing news and Liberal political sentiments almost a century later.

Chesterfield carried on with 'business as usual', and had more luck than some of its neighbours. When cholera broke out in adjoining areas in 1832 the town hurriedly formed a Board of Health, but by sheer good fortune Chesterfield escaped, no cases being reported in the borough. Lucky breaks of this kind could not disguise the basic problem. The town was too small for its growing population, and too heavily reliant on its marketing facility and its craft-style industries. To progress further, Chesterfield needed to join the Industrial Revolution and to expand beyond its own narrow boundaries. The first of these objects would be achieved within a few decades; the latter was to take rather longer. Meanwhile heavy industry thrived in the neighbouring villages and towns, and its own propertied names had begun to move to 'suburban' areas outside the borough to build their impressive Georgian residences. Chesterfield's entrenched, increasingly parochial situation was made all the more evident by the number of dynamic, exceptional men it produced, who had been obliged to leave the borough to make their mark on the national and international stage. Once again, outside was 'where it was happening' and like its most successful sons, Chesterfield would have to look beyond its borders in the years to come.

CHAPTER 8

Star Performers:
Some Georgian Cestrefeldians

Revd John Berridge Jebb. The son of the well-known Joshua Jebb, Revd Jebb was the second incumbent of St Thomas' church, Brampton, from 1846 to 1861. He and his wife lived at Walton Lodge. Described as 'a person decidedly above average ability, who held strong and settled opinions on life, religion and other leading questions', he died in Nice in 1861.

Chesterfield in the Georgian period was notable for producing several eminent figures who went on to establish themselves as internationally famous names. Star pupils of the town's respected grammar school had included the future Archbishop of Canterbury Thomas Secker, the noted antiquary Revd Samuel Pegge who became rector of Whittington, and Caleb Heathcote and Henry Gladwin, of whom more later. Two Chesterfield men became High Sheriffs of Derbyshire, Sir Charles Skrymsher in 1698 and John Bright in 1722. And by the eighteenth century the name of the town was being carried across the world by its association with the Stanhope family, the Earls of Chesterfield.

Philip Stanhope of Shelford and Bretby had been created Earl of Chesterfield by Charles I in 1628. A Derbyshire Royalist who fought for the king in the Civil War, Stanhope had only a tenuous connection with Chesterfield itself, and the same was true of his more famous descendant Philip Dormer Stanhope who became world-famous as Lord Chesterfield. Although only an honorary Cestrefeldian, Lord Chesterfield undoubtedly helped spread awareness of the town to readers of his sayings, and to collectors of coats and furniture bearing his name. Forthright and amusing in his comments, he is nowadays best known for the saying 'never put off until tomorrow what you can do today', but was also quite capable of some *risqué* remarks concerning sex, where he expressed the jaundiced view that 'the position is ridiculous, the pleasure momentary, and the expense damnable'! Sayings aside, Lord Chesterfield also gave his name to the Chesterfield coat and the Chesterfield sofa, both of which have since come in for a fair amount of criticism from experts on fashion and antique furniture, but as has often been said, 'there is no such thing as bad publicity', and these items must also have made more people aware of the town's existence. So, in a roundabout way, Lord Chesterfield probably did his adopted town several useful favours.

If Lord Chesterfield was an adopted figure, Caleb Heathcote was undoubtedly a native son. A descendant of Chesterfield butcher Thomas Heathcote, and a former pupil of the town's grammar school, this remarkable man was one of several brothers involved in international travel and trade. One of his relations, Gilbert Heathcote, was a wealthy merchant with trading interests in India and Jamaica, and Caleb chose the American colonies as his destination. It is claimed that he left his native Derbyshire after being disappointed in love, his prospective bride Mary Dawson jilting him in favour of his elder brother Samuel, a successful merchant. Caleb more than made up for this disappointment by his success in the New World. Arriving in New York in 1692, he quickly showed himself a man of many talents and great entrepreneurial skills. Having served as judge, Colonel of the Westchester County Volunteers, and Surveyor-General of Customs, he made a breakthrough in 1701 when his treaty with local Indian chiefs secured him a rich area which he named the manor of Scarsdale. He held the title of Lord of the Manor of Scarsdale, carrying the name of his native district across the Atlantic, and went on to become Mayor of New York for three successive terms; even more impressively, in the year 1711 Caleb was Mayor of New York while his brother Gilbert was Lord Mayor of London on the far side of the ocean! A devout Anglican, his later years were spent in attempts to spread his religion to Nonconformist Connecticut. Here he enjoyed rather less success, but when he died in 1721 he could look back on a distinguished pioneering career in his new homeland. As a further point of interest, his great-grand-daughter married the famous novelist James Fenimore Cooper, author of *Last of the Mohicans*, who as a tribute to his wife's family wrote a novel entitled *The Heathcotes, or The Wept of Wish-ton-wish*. The district of Scarsdale still exists today, and is regarded as one of the wealthiest areas of Westchester County. Caleb Heathcote carried the name of his home town abroad, and his example pointed the way for others to follow. It is also possible that he may have had some involvement in the naming of Chesterfield in Connecticut, one of eleven Chesterfields in the United States. The tercentenary of his founding of Scarsdale, New York, is to be celebrated in 2001, when American representatives of the former 'manor' are to visit Chesterfield.

Another 'local lad made good' was Henry Gladwin, whose home was at Stubbing Court in Wingerworth, outside the borough, but who like Caleb Heathcote was an alumnus of Chesterfield Grammar School. A member of Derbyshire's landed gentry, Gladwin's father was on friendly terms with the county's biggest landowner, the Duke of Devonshire. The Duke, who in 1792 would establish closer links between the Cavendish family and Chesterfield by buying the manor from his neighbour the Duke of Portland, helped him secure a commission in the British Army. A lieutenant at twenty-three, Henry Gladwin saw service in the American colonies during the Seven Years' War with France, and made some interesting friends. As an officer in the 48th, he accompanied General Braddock's column in its advance on Fort Duquesne, near to modern Pittsburgh. Having crossed the Monongahela River, Braddock and his men were ambushed by a large force of Ottawa, Chippewa and

John Gladwyn Jebb. 'Jack' Jebb, another family member born in Walton, became notable as an explorer, gold prospector, and international entrepreneur. He was a close friend of author H. Rider Haggard, who shared his adventures, and later wrote an introduction to Jack's posthumous biography.

*Caleb Heathcote.
Arguably the most
illustrious of a well-
known local merchant
family, Caleb won fame
in the United States,
where he was lord of
the manor of Scarsdale
in Westchester County,
New York. Three times
Mayor of New York, his
term of office in 1711
also saw his brother
Gilbert become Lord
Mayor of London.*

Potawatomie warriors allied to the French, and suffered a massive defeat, with 400 killed and as many wounded. Others, captured by the ambushers, were tortured to death. Braddock died in the ambush, and Gladwin himself was wounded in the hand and arm, but won praise for his bravery under fire. Another survivor of the battle was George Washington, at that time serving with Lord Murray's regiment and later to become first president of the United States. The story goes that years later Washington would sing 'The Derby Tup' to his grandchildren. Could he have learned it from his fellow officer Henry Gladwin, perhaps?

A good soldier, Gladwin seems to have been unlucky in his choice of commanding officers. After the foolhardy Braddock, he was to serve under the ineffectual General James Abercrombie in his invasion of Canada in 1758. By then Henry had been transferred to the 80th Regiment, a force specially trained, clothed and equipped for wilderness

Village of Scarsdale commemorative plate. Struck by Kettlesprings Kilns of Alliance, Ohio to celebrate the American Bicentenary in 1976, the plate illustrates the agreement of 24 February 1701 between Caleb Heathcote and local Native American chiefs granting him the land for the manor of Scarsdale, New York. Presented to the Derbyshire town, it is now in Chesterfield Museum.

fighting in the Indian manner. Unfortunately Abercrombie made poor use of the men he had, and was soundly defeated by Montcalm at Fort Ticonderoga. He was replaced by General Amherst, who saw Gladwin's qualities and promoted him to Major.

When the Seven Years' War ended, Henry found himself at Fort Detroit (on the site of the modern city), close to the Great Lakes. Unfortunately, it was not long before war was brewing again, as the native Ottawas took exception to the harsh British policies. The result of this tactless severity was a full-scale rebellion led by the Ottawa chief Pontiac, who in 1763 formed an alliance with several other tribes. Pontiac planned a surprise attack on Fort Detroit, but luckily Gladwin was informed of the plot, and the attack was averted. Gladwin and his men held out heroically for the six-month siege that followed, and although other forts were destroyed and their defenders massacred, Fort Detroit stayed in British hands. When it was relieved in 1764, Gladwin was hailed as a hero and promoted to Lieutenant-Colonel. Returning to England and a hero's welcome, he declined active service in America when the War of Independence broke out. Perhaps he had tired of overseas duty, or maybe he did not relish the thought of fighting against George Washington and his other American friends.

The most popular version of events is that Gladwin was informed of Pontiac's plans by an Indian woman, usually referred to as Catherine, and some American historians have claimed that she and Gladwin were on intimate terms. While it has been argued with some justification that Gladwin may have heard the news from several people, and while other claimants have been put forward, it is worth noting that Pontiac and his warriors certainly thought Catherine was responsible, and subjected the poor woman to a beating. This aspect has been largely ignored on our side of the Atlantic, but is it really such an outrageous claim? Henry Gladwin, like many young soldiers serving abroad, could well have made romantic friendships, among which may have been Catherine. If the story is true, then perhaps the romance of Pocahontas and Captain John Smith was re-enacted in eighteenth-century Detroit with a Derbyshire gentleman playing the male lead. Sadly, while Henry was to prosper, Catherine met a tragic end, by falling drunk into a vat of boiling maple syrup.

Henry Gladwin came home to Derbyshire, and passed the remainder of his life at the family home of Stubbing Court as a country gentleman, revered by the public as a war hero and Indian fighter. It is a measure of his celebrity, and no doubt his connections with the Duke of Devonshire, that when the centenary of the 'Glorious Revolution' came round in 1788 it was Henry Gladwin who was chosen to supervise the operations. Given the importance of the Revolution in Protestant British eyes, it was an enormous honour, and no doubt Henry was proud to be chosen.

Just how big an event the centenary was may be indicated by the celebrations that involved Chesterfield and Whittington on 5 November, one hundred years after William III landed at Torbay to claim the throne. A large crowd gathered at Old Whittington, where the rector Revd Samuel Pegge, now aged eighty-four, preached a rousing sermon, which was followed by lunch at the old Cock and Pynot, now renamed the Revolution House. A huge procession then set off from Whittington to Chesterfield, where they were joined by the mayor and corporation. The column is reported to have stretched for a full mile from Whittington Bridge to Stonegravels just north of the town, and to have been 40,000 strong, a number many times greater than the combined populations of Chesterfield and Whittington! Dinner was taken at the three main Chesterfield inns at 4 p.m., and at 6.30 in the evening the day was fittingly celebrated with an impressive display of fireworks in the Market Place. These included what is described as a 'transparent painting' in fireworks of King William III, which must have been worth seeing. This was followed by a ball in the Assembly Room for 300 ladies and

gentlemen. Next day saw a concert and the performance of an ode prepared for the occasion by Revd R. Cunningham of Eyam, and set to music by Chesterfield organist Mr Bower. The scale of the celebrations is staggering, and one can only acknowledge the organizational abilities of Henry Gladwin, who set the whole event in motion. The 1788 Centenary bears all the marks of a carefully planned military campaign, and his was surely the mind behind it. With Caleb Heathcote, he rates as one of Chesterfield's leading Georgians.

If Henry Gladwin and Caleb Heathcote were individuals who caught the eye in Georgian times, then the most successful family of the period is surely that of Jebb. This family arrived in Chesterfield from Mansfield in Nottinghamshire during the early eighteenth century, having already produced some noted figures in the Robin Hood county. Their seventeenth-century ancestor, Samuel Jebb, had won fame as an author and editor of learned works, and one of his sons had a short-lived spell as a baronet, while another perished in the Black Hole of Calcutta. A third son, Joshua, born in 1698, became the patriarch of the Derbyshire clan. Officially described as a hosier, he was married in 1719 at nearby Wingerworth to Mary Woodhouse of Chesterfield. Joshua, who is described as being 'of St Peter's, Nottingham' in the register, was certainly no ordinary tradesman, but a man of substance by the time he came to Chesterfield. Mary Woodhouse was the daughter of John Woodhouse, Esq., of Crich, and this was clearly an advantageous marriage. It marks the beginning of the Derbyshire Jebbs' upward movement from merchants to gentry, a pattern that was followed in later generations. By the mid-eighteenth century Joshua and his family were buying up land from the wealthy Heathcotes inside Chesterfield, and he himself was the owner of Old Hall (later known as Beetwell Hall) on the corner of Beetwell Street and South Place. Joshua Jebb emerged as a leading property owner in the borough, and was made an alderman of Chesterfield. His success set the pace for his sons, who continued to acquire property and status. Joshua, who lived into his 100th year, had plenty of time to appreciate his family's achievements. The Jebbs at this early stage appear to have been Nonconformists; two of Joshua's sons – Avery Jebb and another Joshua – and two of his daughters were baptized at the Unitarian chapel in Elder Yard between 1724 and 1731. As they grew richer, the family followed a well-known pattern, moving out of the borough to imposing residences in the unspoiled 'suburbs'. Avery Jebb built an attractive Georgian house at Tapton Grove in the late eighteenth century, and it was here, or at Walton Lodge, that old Joshua was interviewed by Anna Seward, the Eyam-born poetess known as 'the Swan of Lichfield', before his death in 1797. That he merited an interview from such a celebrity is evidence of Joshua's standing in Chesterfield and beyond.

Another brother, Samuel Jebb, bought the equally impressive Walton Lodge, former home of the wealthy Milnes family, in 1768. The latter part of the eighteenth century saw Jebbs ensconced in suburban mansions to both east and west of the borough, and owners of substantial properties within it.

The Jebbs, like the Heathcotes, were a merchant family, and appear to have been as widely travelled. Samuel Jebb, Joshua's eldest son, is particularly interesting in this respect. In 1752 he married Anne, daughter of William Harriott, Esq., of St Elizabeth, Jamaica, and is himself described as being 'late of Jamaica, now of Chesterfield'. Evidently Samuel had lived in Jamaica, and it seems likely that the family were involved, if not in the slave trade itself, then in the produce of the West Indian sugar plantations. This was an area where vast fortunes were made in the eighteenth century, and it would be surprising indeed if the merchant Jebbs did not obtain at least some of their wealth from this quarter. It may also explain how it was that Samuel's father, the patriarch Joshua, kept a black manservant by the name of Mercury Mallowes, who died in 1803 and is said to be buried in Chesterfield churchyard.

Samuel Jebb was a prominent figure in Chesterfield and Derbyshire public life. Three times mayor of the borough, in 1769, 1774 and 1778, he also served as Deputy Lieutenant of Derbyshire, an appointment that brought him into contact with such notables as the Duke of Devonshire. Together with fellow-merchant Isaac Wilkinson, who was also a partner in the Wilkinson & Jebb banking business, Samuel was a leading figure in the promotion of the Chesterfield Canal, frequently sitting as chairman of the committee. Like his father Joshua he purchased land, much of it outside Chesterfield, including the Walton estate to the west of the borough. A powerful, charismatic personality, Samuel's commercial interests took him far beyond the boundaries of the small, isolated town, into the arena of international trade. His handsome surburban residence at Walton Lodge was further proof of the family's rise in the world.

His brother, Avery Jebb, also married into the gentry, his father-in-law being the owner of Gorse Hall. Avery's country house at Tapton Grove made him a neighbour of Isaac Wilkinson whose home was Tapton House, later to be occupied by railway pioneer George Stephenson. Like his brother Samuel, he took a keen interest in the commercial opportunities offered by the Chesterfield Canal, and in 1801 suggested the laying of a bypass road running directly through from Glumangate in the town centre and across Newbold Road to Wharf Lane, the loading and unloading point for goods on the Canal. The road, part of which would have crossed the site of Holy Trinity church, was never built, but the project indicates the ambition of Avery and his family. Avery's son Richard became a judge in India, while his daughter Marianne married Godfrey Meynell, Esq. of Meynell Langley, further extending the family's position as members of the landed gentry. Samuel Jebb's only son, another Joshua Jebb, married the daughter of the famous Indian fighter and country gentleman Major-General Henry Gladwin, another prestigious match. A colonel in the local Volunteers, Joshua was also a prominent figure in the town, and his death in 1845 brought Chesterfield to a virtual halt, the funeral procession reputedly extending for a mile in length. His burial, under the south transept of St Mary's church, is a fair indication of his importance. Joshua's son became Sir Joshua Jebb KCB, Major-General in the Army, Chairman of Directors of Convict Prisons, Inspector-General of Military Prisons and Surveyor-General of Prisons. This eminent gentleman married the daughter of the attorney W.B. Thomas, of whom more later.

Other family members attained high rank in the Army abroad, one serving as Adjutant-General of India. Another, Walton-born 'Jack' Jebb, became a noted Victorian explorer, whose biography includes an introduction by his friend Rider Haggard, while at a more local level his brother Revd John Berridge Jebb became the second rector of the newly built St Thomas's church in Brampton, a thriving industrial area west of the borough. The achievement of the family was nothing short of phenomenal, and has continued into modern times with the late Lord Gladwyn, a Liberal peer who was Britain's first permanent representative at the United Nations, and who at one time served as Acting Secretary General. By late Victorian times the Jebbs had moved from Derbyshire into Yorkshire, finding eminent careers in their third county of choice. But by that time they had had a major influence on Chesterfield for a century and more.

Last, and by no means least, of this group of luminaries is Wootton Berkinshaw Thomas, who arrived in Chesterfield from Kingston-upon-Thames early in the nineteenth century. Thomas was an attorney, but this description fits the range of his activities no better than 'hosier' serves for Joshua Jebb. He was a man of considerable means, and had an entrepreneur's eye for development potential. Before long he was established as a gentleman farmer at Boythorpe just outside Chesterfield and was breeding short-horned cattle and Merino sheep in the Brampton and Barlow area. He obviously had excellent connections, for King George III (known as 'Farmer George' due to his keen interest in agriculture) in 1810 presented Thomas with two prize Merino ewes. An able publicist, Thomas put on demonstrations of his livestock for neighbouring landowners, and had cloth made from the wool of his flock. He and his wife insisted on wearing clothes made from this home-grown wool. As a cattle breeder, he won the Board of Agriculture's silver cup in 1821 for the best short-horned bull in the United Kingdom. Two years earlier, in 1819, he was the driving force behind the foundation of the Scarsdale and High Peak Agricultural Society, which held some of its meetings in Chesterfield. This body was later to become the Derbyshire Agricultural Society.

In 1825 Thomas bought his own suburban residence when he acquired Highfield from its previous owner Vincent Henry Eyre, for whom Thomas acted as an agent. This Georgian country house, later known as Highfield Hall but then simply as Highfield, lay north of the borough in the parish of Newbold and Dunston, and its purchase confirmed Thomas's arrival as a country gentleman. Apparently a devout churchman, he took on the role of public benefactor in Brampton parish, promoting the building of St Thomas's church and contributing generously towards the costs. The church was built in 1830 on land given by Vincent Henry Eyre through Thomas, his agent.

There were definite connections between W.B. Thomas and the Jebbs. Thomas married a lady from Jamaica who was a ward of the Jebb family, and Revd J.B. Jebb was rector of St Thomas's church in Brampton. Thomas's royal connection with King George III, his agricultural patron, may also have been shared; another member of the Jebb family was the king's physician! As one looks more closely, a network becomes obvious, not only between the Jebbs and Thomas, but including the Gladwin and Heathcote families. All are linked, whether by marriage or by shared commercial and municipal interests, extending to international wealth and trade in America and the Caribbean. In time the net grows wider to include fellow merchant gentry like the Wilkinsons and even George Stephenson, a neighbour of the Jebbs at Tapton House and, like Thomas, a member of the Derbyshire Agricultural Society. While these men lived outside the borough boundaries and their wealth was often gained elsewhere, theirs was a group which greatly influenced most aspects of Chesterfield life throughout the Georgian period and well into the Victorian era. Though often overlooked in previous accounts, there can be no denying their importance to Chesterfield and its history. These were, truly, star performers.

Highfield. Later known as Highfield Hall, the building was home to the Milnes family and later to the Eyres and Manloves. W.B. Thomas, attorney and prize-winning agriculturalist, lived here in the early nineteenth century.

CHAPTER 9

Iron Road, Electric Light:
Victorian Chesterfield

When Victoria came to the throne in 1837 to begin her 'sixty glorious years' as her country's beloved monarch, Chesterfield welcomed in the new era with no obvious outward change. One of England's smallest boroughs at 322 acres, it was scarcely bigger than a farming village, and had advanced hardly at all from its ancient medieval frontiers. Looking at the modern town, a thriving borough and district of over 100,000 people, it is difficult for us to realize just how small Chesterfield was in those days. One sure way of checking is to start from the centre of the Market Place and walk out to north, south, east and west until the old boundaries are reached. Fifteen minutes' steady walking in each direction will bring anyone who cares to try it to the limits of the old borough at Foljambe Road (then known as Pothouse Lane) to the west, Gladstone Road to the north, the river Rother beyond the Midland station to the east, and the site of the old Horns Bridge on Derby Road to the south. For those who believe that Chesterfield has always been a large, populous town, it is a salutary exercise.

The rising population was still crammed into roughly one-third of its space, with more buildings pushed together in the courts and yards, and increasing problems of poor sanitation and disease. Chesterfield was not to find the breathing-space it needed until 1892, almost at the end of the century. All the same the signs were there for those who could read them. By the 1840s, progress was beginning to push harder on those insular boundaries, and would eventually draw a welcome response from the town. Victoria ascended the throne in 1837, succeeding her late uncle William IV. She found herself presiding over a confident, aggressive nation dedicated to ground-breaking inventions and feats of engineering, and already preparing itself for its self-appointed role as ruler of the largest empire the world has ever known. Massive strides were being made in literature and art, and in science and technology. This was the age of Thackeray and Dickens, Tennyson and Browning, Darwin and Faraday, the railway and the telegraph. In the face of such breath-taking progress, even Chesterfield could not remain immune for long.

Most famous of all the Victorian engineers was the railway pioneer George Stephenson, who brought the North Midland Railway to Chesterfield in the early years of Victoria's reign. Its arrival in 1840 marked a new, expansive phase in the development of the town and its region. By no means the first railway engineer, Stephenson had the talent to combine successful working locomotive engines with durable metal railways in a way his rivals failed to equal. With his son Robert, he was already a household name for the triumph of the *Rocket* at the Rainhill Trials, and for overcoming numerous geographic and other problems with the Liverpool-Manchester Railway. George had not originally intended his Derby-Sheffield line to include Chesterfield, but the chance discovery of coal measures at nearby Clay Cross aroused his interest, and he found the town a useful point of access. The North Midland Railway reached Chesterfield in 1840, and the town's first railway station was erected. The line did not so much run through Chesterfield as bypass it on its south-eastern side, skirting the town to the west of the Rother, but was easily accessible to the townspeople, who were quick to make use of

George Stephenson, the famous railway pioneer. His arrival brought the North Midland Railway to the town, and was a factor in its industrial development.

this modern wonder. The railway was a swift, relatively cheap mode of travel and its arrival spelled the end for the Chesterfield Canal, whose use declined as 'railway mania' took over the country. New lines sprang up everywhere, many promoted by the 'Railway King' George Hudson, who made vast profits from the enterprise but was later to suffer a humiliating downfall. Not so George Stephenson, who took the lease of Tapton House from Wilkinson's heir and settled there for the last ten years of his life, keeping a watchful eye on the newly formed Clay Cross Coal and Iron Company while cutting a prominent figure in the life of Chesterfield and Derbyshire as a whole. A bluff, 'self-made' entrepreneur whose North-Eastern accent made him hard for some to understand, Stephenson was forthright in his comments, and was probably not the easiest man to get on with. Many of his fellow-engineers preferred his son Robert, who had a diplomatic talent his father lacked. This said, George undoubtedly made friends in Derbyshire, among them Sir Joseph Paxton, the head gardener at Chatsworth House, and W.B. Thomas, sharing their interest in agriculture and horticulture. In his last years at Tapton House, he made numerous experiments with plants and vegetables, taking great pride in the growing of straight cucumbers with the aid of glass cylinders! When he died in 1848 he was honoured by the town, laid to rest beneath the altar of the recently built Holy Trinity church on Newbold Road. There he lies today, his resting-place marked by a simple plaque with his initials 'G.S.' and the year of his death. A stained-glass window, donated by Robert Stephenson, provides a second attractive memorial. In coming years, the town would further acknowledge its debt with the opening of the Stephenson Memorial Hall on Corporation Street, with the street-name of Stephenson Place, and with well-attended centenary and bicentenary celebrations. Even today Chesterfield Library is besieged by letters from enquirers convinced they are the great man's descendants.

North Midland Railway station. An early illustration of the station, a model of Victorian elegance designed by Francis Thompson, architect to the North Midland Railway Company. Demolished in 1875, the station was replaced by a larger building.

It was only fitting that Chesterfield should honour George Stephenson. His railway helped put the town on the map in the new world of the nineteenth century, bringing visitors, goods and trade to the borough, and providing transport for workers with jobs beyond its boundaries. More significantly, the advent of railways generated further industrial development. In a coal-fired age, railways brought a new market for the iron produced by local forges and furnaces, rails and locomotives were taking over from the cannons and ammunition of the Napoleonic wars, and collieries were essential to provide the required energy. It also provided fresh transport opportunities for goods and services. As the industries of her neighbouring parishes went into overdrive, it was clear that Chesterfield could not remain untouched by the march of progress.

The powerhouse of the surrounding industries was to be found to the west of the borough, in the parish of Brampton. Here a full-blown pottery industry had emerged, with brown ware and stoneware (known as 'Brampton ware') mass-produced in the factories of several large well-established firms, supported by a larger network of collieries, brickworks, clay pits and quarries. Equally significant was the Brampton-based firm of John Bradbury Robinson, which by the mid-nineteenth century was emerging as a large-scale manufacturer of pill-boxes and surgical dressings, while within easy reach of his works near the junction of Chatsworth Road with Wheatbridge Road the Brampton Brewery was turning out the parish's own Brampton ale. Away from Brampton, to the north-east of the borough, the Pearson family ran another pottery at Whittington Moor. The three-village Whittington complex could also boast the glass factory begun by Richard Dixon in the late eighteenth century, although this was soon to close down, while in nearby Sheepbridge the Dunston and Barlow Company, founded in 1856, would metamorphose a few years later into the industrial giant that was the Sheepbridge Coal & Iron Company. Its great rival, the Staveley Company, was already taking shape not far away under the leadership of the Barrow family of ironmasters. Here indeed was the white heat of new technology, and Chesterfield, imprisoned in its centre, was inevitably affected by the events all around.

Its primary function was still as a centrally situated market town, and then as now the Market Place was one of its most striking features. The old medieval square gained an impressive ornament in 1857 with the opening of the Market Hall. A tall, imposing brick structure in the Italianate manner, designed by Messrs Davies & Tew, it was erected by the private Chesterfield Market Hall Company in a central position, dividing the main market-place from New Square. Built to accommodate the public on wet market days, it proved multi-functional, with separate sectors marked out for corn and butter markets, assembly rooms and a new home for the court house. The Market Hall was lambasted by critics almost from the beginning, and came in for severe criticism when a general antipathy to Victorian buildings took hold in the early twentieth century, but it still stands today, albeit refurbished, having served the people of Chesterfield well for nearly a century and a half. Sight of the tall, striking edifice gleaming in the sunlight on fine days must have impressed many visitors to the town, and no doubt still does.

All the same, tall new buildings failed to hide the rustic nature of the market itself. New Square, formerly known as Swine's Green, was the regular herding-place for livestock awaiting sale and slaughter, and market-days in the town must have blended a rich variety of sounds and scents, not all of them pleasant. Writing soon after the end of Victoria's reign, Pendleton and Jacques provide a lively description of those former days: 'Before the opening of the new Cattle Market two years ago, the Market-place on Saturday and on fair-day resembled a huge farm-yard. Horses, cattle, sheep, pigs, drovers and agriculturists thronged every street that led into the town from the country, and around the north, west and south sides of the Market Hall, and along High Street and in the New Square and West

The Shambles, looking towards the Market Place, in the 1880s. An area used by butchers and other tradesmen from medieval times, the Shambles in the Victorian era typified the overcrowding, crime, filth and disease afflicting the centre of town.

Bars, nearly every man had a bit of straw in his mouth, or a stick cut from the "plantin", or a whip in his hand… and many a shrewd bargain was driven either in the square or in an adjacent inn, while the irresponsible bull or milch cow clattered through the doorway of the first shop it strayed to, to get inextricably mixed up with the stock, or hopelessly jammed behind the counter.'

Evidently being a shopkeeper in Chesterfield was not without its dangers. The Market Hall was one of several public buildings erected in Chesterfield during the Victorian era. If not immediately convinced by the benefits of industry, the town fathers were prepared to make improvements to the borough and its amenities. The grammar school, which over the past few years had fallen into neglect, was rebuilt in 1846 and its fortunes were revived under its new headmaster, the Revd Frederick Calder, while the following year a Municipal Hall was built at the corner of the Bowling Green for carrying out corporation business. Gas street lighting was installed and a water supply established by the Chesterfield Gas & Water Company, drawing on reservoirs at Linacre to the west of the borough, although increasing demand meant the constant building of fresh reservoirs at the site. The restructuring of the Poor Law legislation saw the appointment of a Board of Guardians and the building of a new workhouse on Newbold Road in 1840; this was run not by the corporation but by a body known as the Vestry, whose remit was based on the much larger Chesterfield ecclesiastical parish rather than the 300 acres of the borough. The new Royal Hospital was erected in 1859 on the corner of Holywell Street, on the site of the medieval Durrant Hall, and further extensions to the building were made at the turn of the century.

The Chesterfield School Board was set up in 1871 in response to the Education Act of the year before; the corporation was one of the first authorities to adopt this Act, which was devised to combat the widespread illiteracy in the country as a whole. Schools were built at central locations in Hipper Street and Hollis Lane, and in the north of the borough on St Helen's Street and Durrant Road. These added to existing Georgian schools such as the Victoria Schools on Vicar Lane and the School of

Market Hall, Market Place. Designed in the Italianate style by Messrs Davies & Tew, the hall was erected in 1857 as a covered area for market users, and divided into corn and butter markets, assembly room and court house. Often criticized in its early days, the refurbished building is now seen as an attraction for tourists.

Industry, where 'the daughters of the poor' were trained in the basics for a future as domestic servants. The Stephenson Memorial Hall on Corporation Street, opened by the Duke of Devonshire in 1879, combined a memorial to the railway pioneer with a free library, lecture hall, theatre and science and art classes. Later still, the revamped grammar school took on another role, serving as a venue for technical education and university extension classes in the evenings.

Perhaps the most startling innovation was the borough's adoption of electric street lighting in 1881. This came about as the result of a squabble over the future terms of a new lighting contract by the Gas & Water Company, which shut off the light for a month in September of that year. The problems caused by people blundering about the darkened streets of town, and the complaints that resulted, led the corporation to take up the offer of Messrs Hammond & Co. to give a three-week trial of the electric system. Eight arc lamps were installed in the centre of town, the dynamo driven by an 8hp engine located in the Theatre Royal in Theatre Yard. It proved a success, and the corporation signed a contract for the town to be lit for another year by twenty-two arc lights and fifty Lane-Fox incandescent lamps. The scheme was in place by the summer of 1882, and generated interest throughout the country; a number of experts visited the town and went away impressed by what they saw. There has been some dispute over whether or not Chesterfield can fairly claim to be the first town lit by electricity. Godalming, its main rival, also adopted electric lighting in 1881 a few days earlier, using a water-powered system, but while the Chesterfield scheme succeeded Godalming's system proved a short-lived failure. So, Chesterfield can certainly claim to be the first town *successfully* lit by electricity. Unfortunately the honeymoon period with Hammond & Co. did not last long. The company was not making an economic return from lighting the streets, and wanted to run further wires for the more profitable lighting of shops and houses in the town. The corporation drew the line at this, and the agreement lapsed. The Gas & Water Company returned with more favourable terms, and Chesterfield reverted to gaslight in 1884. It was a sad postscript to what had been a daring experiment.

If electric lighting was the most unusual innovation in Victorian Chesterfield, the most significant new arrivals were the large number of Irish workers and their families who made an important contribution to the life of the town. Detailed research by Derek Topp has exploded a number of popular myths about this community. They were by no means all railway workers on the North Midland Railway as was previously supposed; in fact most of them arrived between 1840 and 1850, and were employed in a variety of occupations. Nor did they live grouped together in segregated 'ghetto' areas in the centre of town. There were Irish living in the cramped courts and yards off Low Pavement, including the slum area known as the 'Dog Kennels', but an equal number were distributed in other parts of the town. They appear to have adapted quickly to their new circumstances, becoming an integral part of the community.

Like the French prisoners of war a generation earlier, the Irish were mostly of the Roman Catholic faith, and like most 'foreign' newcomers were no doubt viewed with suspicion at first. The Victorian

The Vicarage, Church Way, in a view from early in the last century, by C.H. Nadin. The vicarage garden occupied a large acreage between Church Way and Vicar Lane, and in the 1990s was the site of archaeological excavations which found evidence of Roman settlement. The area is now part of the Vicar Lane shopping development.

Displayed on the Elizabethan town seal and now superseded, this early version of the Borough Arms derives from that used by the common council in 1480. The central emblem of the pomegranate tree 'eradicated' and 'fructed' (uprooted and bearing fruit) is a rarely used heraldic device which still appears on the present-day arms.

View of Chesterfield from Hady, east of the town. Taken from an early nineteenth century oil painting.

South-west view of Chesterfield, 1812, from an old print of a watercolour painting, possibly an early work by George Pickering (1794-1857).

Spital House, near Chesterfield, 1812, from an old print of a watercolour painting also credited to George Pickering. Spital House, erected by Gervase Shaw in 1574 on the site of old monastic buildings, was home to several notable local families before being demolished in the 1950s.

Left: *Jonas Chapman's 1837 map of Chesterfield, showing the small, confined area of the old borough, which was not to increase its size and population until 1892.* Right: *Medieval grave, discovered in the garden of a house in June 2000. The remains are thought to be of a twelfth-century priest, who ministered to the inmates of the nearby St Leonard's Leper Hospital from which the district of Spital takes its name.*

Formal reburial service for the exhumed priest, at Spital Cemetery, 24 April 2001.

West House, West Bars, 1894-95 from a painting by Col. J. Kinsman, presented to Chesterfield Library by his nephew Lt. Col. T.H. Barnes, who was born there in 1896. West House was, at different times, home to the Maynards, to Harold Soames and his daughter Olave (later Lady Baden Powell), and afterwards to Lt- Col. Barnes and his parents.

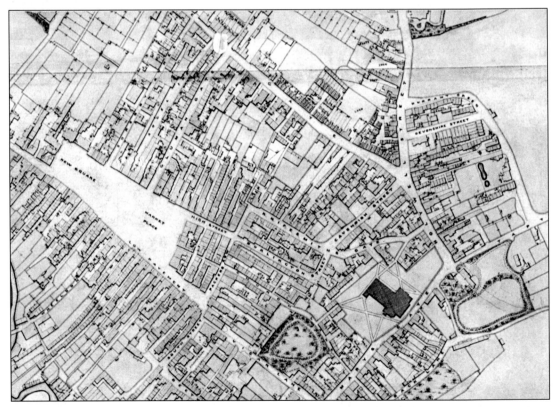

Section from a map by Charles Robertson, c. 1850, showing the Market Place and New Square as a large open area with the Shambles on its eastern side. The Market Hall was to appear later, in 1857. On the far right is the parish church of St Mary and All Saints, and below it is the large vicarage garden.

Left: *Royal Oak Inn, the Shambles. Part of the medieval town centre, the inn is said to have been a rest house for the Knights Templar. It occupies the site of a much older building, but has been altered, and possibly rebuilt in 1748. Known as the 'Hollybush' and 'Pluto's Palace' in earlier days, the inn was restored in 1898-99, the original timber being carefully preserved. Right: Royal Oak sign, the familiar version with a portrait of Charles II.*

Royal Oak sign, stating its early use as a medieval resting place for the Knights Templar of nearby Temple Normanton.

Chesterfield Market Place. One of the largest open markets in the country when first laid out in the thirteenth century, the Market Place has remained the focus for traders and visitors for hundreds of years, and into the new millennium.

Chesterfield, a modern view from Hady Hill. As always, the spire of the parish church dominates the landscape. The white building in the right foreground houses the offices of the Derbyshire Times.

Miners' offices, Saltergate.

Statues of miners' MPs, Saltergate. Statues of W.E. Harvey (left) and James Haslam (right), fronting the NUM offices on Saltergate. Both men were leading Chesterfield trade unionists who served as miners' MPs early in the twentieth century. Haslam represented Chesterfield and Harvey North East Derbyshire.

Barnett Observatory, Hastings Close, Newbold. Designed by local enthusiast Horace Barnett and his colleagues, the observatory was opened by the Astronomer Royal in 1960.

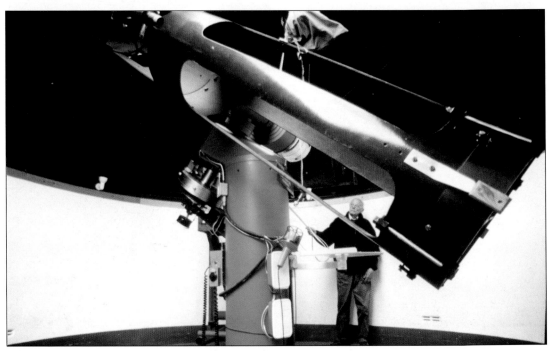

Inside the Barnett Observatory. Now fully updated with computerized equipment, it still contains the excellent 18in telescope designed by Horace Barnett and his friends in the late 1950s.

Prince Charles and Princess Diana appear on the balcony of the Market Hall to the cheers of the crowds during their visit to Chesterfield in 1981, when they opened the Pavements Shopping Centre.

The Market Hall clock tower in 2001. A permanent fixture since 1857, it dominates the Market Place as the Crooked Spire does the town itself, and adds its own Victorian character to the medieval market square.

Left: *Christina Murrell Wade. An assistant in Chesterfield Library, Christina was born in Chesterfield to parents who came here from Grenada. A talented artist whose work has been exhibited locally, she studies at Sheffield Hallam University, where she has also appeared in student films. Her award-winning sculpture is displayed in Sheffield Cathedral.* Right: *Jackson's Bakers, Low Pavement. Operating from premises on one of Chesterfield's most historic streets, Jackson's Bakers (formerly 'Something Special') has for several years proved a popular venue for both locals and visitors.*

The Peacock. Now the town's tourist information centre, its site has been occupied from medieval times. The present building dates from the Tudor period, and was first known as the Peacock Inn in the eighteenth century. A listed building, it is also a venue for exhibitions, and well dressings are held annually in the old inn yard.

Wok 2000, a more recent arrival and close neighbour to the Peacock on Low Pavement.

The Herbal Inn, which offers acupuncture and Chinese herbal medicine, in the Vicar Lane shopping centre.

The Tuminose Kebab and Grill House on Cavendish Street makes a further contribution to Chesterfield's multi-cultural cuisine.

Vicar Lane. The new shopping area, viewed from the town centre and looking towards St Mary's Gate.

Bowling Green, Beetwell Street/South Place. One of the oldest Chesterfield landmarks, the site was conveyed as a gift by Richard II to the Guild of the Virgin Mary and Holy Cross in 1392. Sold by Sir Thomas Foljambe to the corporation in 1604, its history was recorded by local tradesman George Lee in 1913.

Markham Road. This street has seen marked changes in the last few years, its housing replaced by the stores of the Ravenside Retail Park. At the far end of the road, Focus Do-it-All occupies the site of the demolished Queen's Park Hotel.

Alma Leisure Complex, Derby Road, showing the Cannon Gymnasium, and to its right the Cineworld multiplex cinema. Just off the main roundabout at Derby Road, the centre is one of several significant new developments in the town.

The road eastward out of Chesterfield, looking towards Hady Hill, at the eastern boundary of the old borough. On the left is the sign for Piccadilly Road, where the skeleton of the priest was found in a nearby garden. On the right, shaded by trees, is Spital Cemetery where he was recently reburied.

Medieval Market, July 2001. This annual fair and market has become an eagerly awaited date in the local calendar, and is always well attended.

The Crooked Spire. The twisted spire of the parish church, Chesterfield's most familiar landmark, viewed from below. Probably the result of heat on leaden tiles and unseasoned wooden framework, the 228 foot spire has evoked many legends and verses, and has come to symbolize the enduring nature of the town itself.

THE "LANE-FOX" INCANDESCENT LIGHT IN THE CHURCHYARD

THE "ARC" LIGHT IN ST. MARY'S GATE

Electric lighting at Chesterfield: an illustration from the Graphic *of 1882, showing the pioneering installation of electric arc and incandescent lighting around the parish church. Chesterfield made the change from gas to electric lighting in October 1881, and may fairly claim to be the first town successfully lit by electricity.*

Englishman tended to see himself as part of an innately superior 'Anglo-Saxon' Protestant civilization, an image generated by the 1688 Revolution and fed by empire-builders like Charles Kingsley, Carlyle and others, and the incoming Irish were no doubt on the receiving end of this prejudice. The *Derbyshire Times*, in an early editorial of the 1850s, responded to a minor disturbance in the town with a diatribe on 'The Unruly Irish' that would be greeted with horror in our own time. And what the newspaper printed, many Chesterfield people probably secretly thought, whether they actually said so or not. Something of this feeling seems to have surfaced in 1862, when the arrival of the so-called Baron

An old Georgian lodging house, at the junction of Beetwell Street and Lordsmill Street. Chesterfield's lodging houses were severely criticized as hotbeds of disease and squalor in the nineteenth century. This 1950s scene, prior to demolition, shows the house covered with posters advertising household products.

Lordsmill Street, viewed from the junction with Markham Road. The rutted road and unprepossessing buildings presented a grim prospect typical of the nineteenth-century town, but have since been replaced.

de Camin sparked disorder in the town. A rabid anti-Catholic lecturer who would nowadays be dismissed as a crank, he was certainly no baron, and his alleged 'real name' of André Massena (a famous Marshal of France) also seems dubious. Large numbers of Irish people gathered to object to his proposed speech, and he had to be smuggled out of the town. There was a violent disturbance and some protestors were injured before the crowd was dispersed by a charge of the local volunteers. No doubt some animosity lingered after the event.

Hard-line Protestant attitudes were still alive in Chesterfield in the 1880s and were once again expressed in the bicentenary celebrations for the Glorious Revolution, although the late staging of the event suggests that they had less support than in the previous century. An incident with more dangerous potential repercussions was the Phoenix Park assassination of 1882, when Fenian activists shot dead Lord Frederick Cavendish and his secretary in Dublin. The murder of a Cavendish, relative of Derbyshire's 'spiritual leader' of the Protestant cause, the Duke of Devonshire, could have had unpleasant consequences in Chesterfield. This time, however, violence was avoided, the town worthies and the people expressing their condolences and attending a large but peaceful public meeting in support of the Duke and his bereaved family.

It is greatly to the credit of the Irish workers that they overcame the entrenched attitudes of their hosts, and over a period of years became an important part of the community. Their need for a place of worship was fulfilled by the Jesuit fathers of Spinkhill, who founded the church of St Mary and the Annunciation on Spencer Street in 1854. Presently they would make further contributions to the town's public life by producing individuals like Chesterfield's Chief Constable Robert Kilpatrick, while for its first half-century the Free Library would be run by Dennis Gorman and George MacMahon, both of them worshippers at Spencer Street.

CHAPTER 10

A Darker Side:
the Borough Below the Surface

Public health was the overriding problem for Chesterfield in the nineteenth century. A growing population, most of it packed into a medieval core of buildings, the courts and yards with their insanitary conditions, contributed to the spread of disease. The town was plagued by high infant mortality, mostly caused by diarrhoea in the hot summer months, and there were frequent outbreaks of typhoid and other infectious diseases. The Victorian fathers made efforts to combat the situation, directing their energies to the disposal of sewage. Seven filter beds were set up in strategic parts of the town in 1873, while in 1878 the corporation purchased a site near Lockoford Lane outside the borough in Newbold parish to install a sewage farm and its outfall. These were genuine attempts at improvement, but the Borough's Medical Officer of Health pointed out that they were doomed to failure. The outlying parishes, less environmentally minded on this occasion than Chesterfield, were flooding the River Rother not only with sewage but with effluent from their burgeoning industries, and this wholesale pollution was more than enough to negate the borough's own efforts. Not until Chesterfield extended its boundaries to unite with its immediate neighbours would this problem be effectively tackled.

The truth of the matter is that beneath Chesterfield's worthy veneer of public works, and advances in welfare and education, the town itself was a hotbed of vice, crime, filth and disease. The problems it shared with other Victorian market towns were made all the more shocking by the small size of the borough, where a growing population was pushed together in a confined 100 acres of habitation. It seems fair to argue that Chesterfield's largest unacknowledged industry was that of brewing beer. As long ago as 1697 Celia Fiennes had remarked that 'here is the finest ale in the kingdom generally esteem'd', and by the 1850s the borough was served by three large local breweries, two of them in the town itself. The Brampton Brewery sat at the western edge of the town, just outside the boundary but well within reach, while the Scarsdale Brewery on Spa Lane and the Chesterfield Brewery at the junction of Brimington Road and Infirmary Road supplied their wares from inside the town. And there was no shortage of outlets for them.

Bagshaw's trades directory of 1846, which praises Chesterfield as 'an extensive market and borough town…pleasantly situated on an eminence, between the rivers Rother and Hipper', also lists no less than forty-six 'hotels, inns and taverns' there; by 1872, Francis White's directory notes a startling increase, with sixty-seven hotels, inns and taverns, backed up by fifty-four beerhouses, the vast majority of which are crammed into the inhabited third of the 300-acre town itself. Such a concentration of drinking-places, in such a small area, is staggering to contemplate. And while there is nothing wrong with either breweries or public houses in themselves, the state of central Chesterfield at night can only be imagined. That there was regular drunkenness and violent rowdiness there we know from the court reports in the local press; from them we also learn that some of the drinking establishments offered other, more sordid, services to their customers. Child prostitution was a national scandal in Victorian

times, and there is no reason to suppose that Chesterfield was any exception. The 1851 census entry for Low Pavement, for example, includes four women who give their profession as that of 'prostitute', and it seems a fair bet that there were many more involved in the same trade who were not prepared to admit it. Squalid transactions took place in the unlit yards off the Market Place, where sometimes violence escalated to murder. In 1845 the body of George Collis was found in a cesspool near Bunting's Yard in the Shambles. He had been battered to death with a spade, wielded by John Platts, who owed him money. Platts was convicted, and paid the ultimate penalty. While this is obviously an extreme example, it was far from being the only incident of its kind. As for the effect of heavy drinking on domestic violence, in an age when doors were closed on private lives, the true extent will probably never be known. Drinking, a pleasant pastime to most, was the source of fortunes for some. As a result, one cannot help feeling that a blind eye was often turned to its less pleasant consequences. This dark underside to Victorian Chesterfield has rarely found its way into histories of the town, but was nevertheless very much a part of daily life at the time.

There is no shortage of evidence for the grim state of the town. On 1 July 1871 the *Derbyshire Courier* carried a paragraph from the renowned medical journal *The Lancet*, where the writer castigated the borough and its inhabitants in no uncertain terms. Declaring that 'The sanitary state of [Chesterfield] is anything but satisfactory' he went on to remark that:

> 'There is a polluted river, defective drainage and the town possesses no baths and wash-houses and no cattle market. The Chesterfield Town Council should bestir itself. The river Rother ought no longer to be polluted by sewage which might easily be turned to account in irrigating land at a sufficient distance from the town to prevent it becoming a nuisance. Chesterfield, we believe, is prospering and increasing in population and there is every reason, therefore, why the streets should not be turned into a cattle market, and some attention should be given to the subject of public wash-houses and baths.'

Even more salutary was the report of Dr Thorne, a medical expert with a national reputation who was engaged to investigate the state of public health in the town. When he gave his findings to the corporation in January 1874, the doctor spared neither the town nor its leaders, and his report makes shocking reading today. Thorne lists an appalling catalogue of filth and disease for which no remedy had been found. Out of every 100 children born, 15 would die before they were a year old, compared with the average death-rate of 12 per 100, and many of these were victims of diarrhoea and typhoid – deaths which could have been prevented. Both diseases were 'intimately connected' to 'the conditions of sewage and excrement and refuse disposal.' Sewage was being passed into the Rother, and 'no one could for a moment suppose that was a proper means of disposal.' With regard to the removal of excrement and refuse: 'This nuisance had assumed gigantic proportions. He had visited scores of places where the middens had been filled to overflowing, and outside there were as many as ten cartloads of filth. Some of the closets could not be approached because of the accumulation, and in the inside the contents of the closets rose a foot above the seats.' The sole means of sewer ventilation was through the rain spouts on the houses, which Dr Thorne rightly pointed out was a further means of spreading disease to those inside. He went on to provide a horrifyingly graphic description of large numbers of people packed into filthy, sub-standard housing regardless of their age or sex. The lodging houses in particular had left their mark on the good doctor: 'He did not think they could find a town in the kingdom to equal Chesterfield in regard to lodging houses. There were some circumstances in a person's lifetime which could never be forgotten, and he should never in his life forget his midnight visit to the Chesterfield lodging houses. If he were to describe the conditions he found prevailing in defiance of every consideration of both decency and health… it would necessitate the use of language better avoided… the foul sights of Chesterfield were scars in his memory forever.'

Harsh words indeed, and obviously they were uttered none too soon. If Chesterfield was to grow and develop it was clear it would have to break out of these restrictive boundaries which threatened in time to reduce the place to a cesspit. In fairness to them, there were men on the corporation who realized the necessity, and efforts to extend the borough were made from the 1870s onwards. They encountered resistance from diehards who dreaded the possibility of increased costs, and from the industrialized parishes outside who were unwilling to give up their independence. Although logic was on the side of the borough leaders, who were already providing services to those outside through the School Board, the Hospital and the Poor Law Union, their first attempt was rejected by the Government Commission as 'not proven' in 1876, but a more concerted campaign was mounted in 1891, and the following year the vital breakthrough was made.

The borough boundary was extended to take in the large industrial parish of Brampton and the Brockwell district of Newbold. Overnight Chesterfield found itself doubled in size and almost in population, with all the industrial production of the western potteries and collieries added to its armoury. One late and important convert was William Bradbury Robinson, head of the packaging firm, who was so shocked by the desperate state of the sewers that he campaigned strongly for the extension he had previously opposed. With the election of the new Borough Council, the leadership of Chesterfield saw a radical change, the shopkeepers, brewers and minor officials being joined by several industrial entrepreneurs, not only W.B. Robinson but Charles P. Markham of the Staveley Company and later of Markham & Co. Ltd, and the Plowright brothers who headed the Brampton engineering firm. For the first time in its history, Chesterfield looked beyond 300 acres to take on a wider vision. The town had finally come of age.

Chesterfield Borough Council in 1893. The mayor is W.B. Robinson, head of the Brampton packaging firm. From left on the front row are W.O. Plowright, T.P. Wood and J.M. Clayton. Dr George Booth and Edward Woodhead are at the far right. Paul Bradley, the town crier and mace bearer, stands on the left.

CHAPTER 11

Leading Lights:
More Chesterfield Victorians

For obvious reasons, George Stephenson has usually captured the headlines for Chesterfield's Victorian period. While he is more than worthy of his place, other Cestrefeldians are deserving of mention, and a few of these appear below.

James Abercrombie had his home outside the borough at Stubbing Court, Wingerworth, a residence previously occupied by 'Indian fighter' Henry Gladwin and later home to Harold Soames, owner of the Brampton Brewery and father of Lady Olave Baden Powell. A pupil at Chesterfield Grammar School, Abercrombie later presided at meetings of Chesterfield's Philosophical Society. He made his name in politics, becoming an MP, and in 1835 was appointed Speaker of the House of Commons, in spite of the opposition of Sir Robert Peel. He was raised to the peerage as Lord Dunfermline in 1839. His name is celebrated in the town by Abercrombie Street off Newbold Road, a short distance from Stephenson's resting place at Holy Trinity church.

Francis Frith was born in Chesterfield in 1822, son of a well-known Quaker family who had lived in the area for over 200 years. Frith left his home town as a young man to make his way in the world. He became a leading figure in the world of photography, setting up his firm of Francis Frith & Co. in Reigate, Surrey, in 1859. Frith helped to pioneer location photography, producing postcard series and albums of photographs of Britain's towns and villages – including his native town of Chesterfield – and also ventured to more exotic regions. At considerable risk to himself, he was the first photographer to travel down the Nile and across desert terrain to photograph the Pyramids of Egypt, his bulky cameras and precious photographic plates carried by a team of mules. Frith overcame these and other difficulties, fighting off attacks by robbers and wild dogs, in between taking the vital pictures. Using three types of camera, including a dual stereoscopic lens that provided a three-dimensional effect, he brought home some of the earliest images of these monuments to the pharaohs ever seen in this country. His company continued in business until late in the twentieth century, and its vast collection of photographs has only recently been sold. Commemorative albums of Frith's work are currently available through commercial publishers.

Samuel Rollinson, another Chesterfield Grammar School alumnus, began his work for the Chesterfield Corporation as Sanitary Inspector in 1864. His was an unenviable task, but he performed well under difficult circumstances before leaving to begin a more impressive career as an architect. Rollinson designed and restored several churches in Chesterfield and north-east Derbyshire, notably St Laurence, Barlow (1867), Christ Church, Stonegravels (1868), St Peter and Paul, Brampton (1869), St Peter, Calow (1887) and Holy Trinity church on Newbold Road (1888-89). For some years architect to the Duke of Devonshire, he was a Chesterfield Borough Councillor from 1880 to 1891, and his family firm of Rollinson & Son at 13 Corporation Street was an institution in the town.

Francis Augustus Hatton sparked off something of a 'newspaper war' when he founded the *Derbyshire Times* in Chesterfield in 1854. The first penny newspaper in the county, the *Times* struggled in its early years and Hatton experienced financial difficulties that may have contributed to his sudden death in 1855. The business was kept in operation by his widow and their son William Hatton, and in later years by Wilfred and W.H. Edmunds, and its Conservative viewpoint provided a lively rivalry with the Liberal *Derbyshire Courier*, until the latter was taken over by the *Times* in 1922. Another of Hatton's sons, Joseph, became the celebrity of the family. Joseph Hatton made his name as editor of the *Gentleman's Magazine* in the 1860s, owned and edited the *Sunday Times*, and wrote as drama critic for the *Observer* and as London correspondent of the *New York Times*. He also secured a major scoop with his report on President Garfield's assassination for the *Standard* in 1881. Joseph spent his last seven years as editor-in-chief of *The People* from 1900 to 1907. As a younger man he won fame as a novelist with such works as *The Banishment of Jessop Blythe*, *By Order of the Czar* and *Three Recruits*, the last of which draws on his experiences in Chesterfield. Hatton often visited Chesterfield, where he was popular as a public reader of his novels. He made his reading debut at the newly built Stephenson Memorial Hall in October 1879.

Thomas Philpot Wood Jr was both a prominent citizen and a local character. His family had lived in Chesterfield from early in the nineteenth century, but originated from Sevenoaks in Kent. T.P. Wood attended the grammar school and also studied abroad before returning to his home town to enter the family business as a wine and spirit merchant. His premises on High Street fronted on to the Market Place, and were later taken over for the Littlewoods store. He also diversified into the popular production of mineral water and cigars, and compiled his now famous *Almanac* as a yearly gift to his customers. A lively concoction of local information, a calendar of events and jokes of the Christmas cracker variety, it continued in being up to his death in 1911 and was later revived, finally disappearing in the 1960s. An invaluable source to librarians and enquirers for the history of local organizations and events, it still makes an entertaining read today. T.P. Wood was three times Mayor of the borough, his most famous year of office being 1887, when he supervised the founding of his brainchild, Queen's Park, to celebrate Victoria's Golden Jubilee. Fields belonging to E.G. Maynard and known as 'Maynard's Meadows' were purchased, with funds partly raised by T.P. Wood himself, who held parties at his home at Brambling House on Hady Hill. The park was formally dedicated on 21 September 1887, when celebrations took place in the town and a procession of horse-drawn tableaux showing Chesterfield's trades and businesses paraded through the park and posed for the photographers. It was not officially opened until 1893, when it hosted the first Chesterfield & District Agricultural and Horticultural Society show. As the park was usually declared 'closed'

Thomas Philpot Wood Jr. Born at Boythorpe House, T.P. Wood was a wine and spirits merchant in the town, whose annual almanacs provide a wealth of local information. Three times Mayor of Chesterfield, he is best known as founder and fund-raiser for Queen's Park, established in 1887 as a tribute to Victoria's Golden Jubilee.

William Bradbury Robinson. Son of J.B. Robinson, who founded the Brampton packaging firm, W.B. Robinson visited the United States before returning to expand the business; Wheatbridge Mills became the first surgical dressings factory in the world. A member of Brampton & Walton Council and Brampton School Board, he joined the Borough Council following extension, and was Mayor of Chesterfield in 1893 and 1894.

to all but the Society, it was open and closed at the same time, a fact which caused great amusement in the press. Queen's Park boasted a cricket ground, bowling green and boating lake, together with other features such as the bandstand and the conservatory with its array of plants. W.G. Grace played cricket there on two occasions in the 1900s, and county matches were played on the ground until the 1990s. The park has hosted a wide range of sporting and leisure activities ever since, from cricket and bowls matches to school sports, Sunday School demonstrations, band concerts and the 1919 Peace Celebrations. A worthy monument to its founder, it is still Chesterfield's main, and most attractive, leisure facility. It paved the way for more parks and leisure projects in other parts of the borough in following years. Aside from the medieval Bowling Green, the main sporting venue to predate Queen's Park is the Recreation Ground on Saltergate, on which W.G. Grace also played in 1871, and which became the home ground for Chesterfield Football Club.

As characters go, few can have been more memorable or endearing than Dennis Gorman, the Irish Roman Catholic ex-police officer who became Chesterfield's first librarian. His early life is something of a mystery, beyond the fact that he was born in Ireland (he never says exactly where on the census returns!) and that he joined the Derbyshire Constabulary not long after its formation in 1856. The new Derbyshire force drew heavily on the Royal Irish Constabulary for officers, and Gorman would have found himself working with many of his former countrymen, if not co-religionists. As a Sergeant, he took an active role in investigating the Ashover murder of 1857 that was probably the Constabulary's first big murder case, and made an arrest. The suspect was released for lack of evidence, but Gorman was commended and went on to make Inspector at Clay Cross before being appointed Superintendent of the Eckington Division. Here, in 1870, he came close to losing his life in pursuit of his duty, when he made the single-handed arrest of a sheepstealer near Beighton. The poacher turned on Gorman and fired a pistol point-blank, peppering his face and shoulder with shot and blinding him with the gunflash. A struggle ensued, the criminal pulling a knife and biting Gorman who despite heavy loss of blood hung on to his adversary. Luckily others came to the rescue, the man was apprehended and received a life sentence. For a time it was touch and go whether Gorman would survive, but he came through his ordeal, which left him with impaired sight in one eye and pain and discomfort for the rest of his life. Honourably discharged from the force, he re-appeared in Chesterfield in 1879, when he was appointed 'Hall-keeper and librarian' at the Stephenson Memorial Hall on Corporation Street.

The Memorial Hall had been opened with full Masonic honours by the Duke of Devonshire on 14 July 1879. It was intended to serve a twofold purpose; as a memorial to George Stephenson, and as an educational and social venue. University extension classes in science and art were held there, making use of purpose-built laboratory and art room facilities, there was a lecture hall and theatre, and the building also housed the libraries of the local Mechanics Institute and the rather more elite Institute of Engineers as well as Chesterfield's Free Public Library. The Memorial Hall Committee had strained their resources to the limit to have the building erected, and there was no money for stock. (One of Gorman's first complaints was 'I am a librarian without books!')

Generous donations overcame this problem, and when the library finally opened in 1880 Gorman had material for his customers. Although not a qualified librarian – few were in those days – he adapted remarkably well to his new post, showing a keen awareness of the value of local history material and of children's literature in his reports and appeals for donations. A bold, combative figure not afraid to speak his mind, his relationship with his employers was often stormy, but he clearly commanded respect and affection from the Chesterfield public. When the Corporation bought the Hall in 1889, he changed masters but the relationship was much the same. In 1896 a fierce row erupted when Gorman was required to light and extinguish the gas in the library, a menial task to which he reacted with outraged dignity. His protests to the Library Committee unavailing, he wrote angrily to the *Derbyshire Times* with a letter that raises a smile today, airing his oratorical skill with some classical allusions: 'Andromeda was chained to a rock, Sisyphus is doomed to keep rolling his huge stone up the hill, and the Chesterfield librarian is bound to twelve gas burners!' Quite rightly carpeted by the Committee chairman for this outburst, Gorman had no more to say, but verbal warfare broke out everywhere else. In the press, letters poured in for the next two or three months, most of them taking Gorman's side and expressing outrage that 'one who has grown grey in the service' should be subjected to such indignity. This storm in a gaslight finally blew itself out in a series of Committee meetings where the majority, though not condoning Gorman's actions, felt he had been unfairly treated. In the end the chairman resigned his post while Gorman stayed on, serving the Chesterfield public for thirty years until his death in 1909 at

Boating Lake, Queen's Park. A post-war view by the late Fred Jacques.

Decorated flower bed in the park, commemorating the local Sherwood Foresters regiment.

the age of seventy-nine, by which time most of the other organizations had left the Hall while the successful library extended its premises. Mourned as 'an old and valued servant' by the corporation and the Chesterfield public, he was succeeded by his friend and assistant George MacMahon, a fellow Irishman and member of the Spencer Street church. Dennis Gorman is buried in the Spital Cemetery in a shared, unpurchased grave which lacks any indication of who lies there. Joint attempts by the police and library service to raise a monument to him failed to materialize, but it is surely high time that one should be found for a man who served them both with such distinction.

Unlike his chief, MacMahon was born in Chesterfield to an Irish immigrant family, his father a colliery labourer from Limerick and his mother hailing from County Mayo. Raised in poor, crowded accommodation in Britt's Court in the town centre, he worked for the Sheepbridge Company before taking on his new post, where he served the public ably until his premature death in 1921. His daughter Catherine was later to have a long career as an assistant in the library.

Spital Cemetery is also the burial place for Chesterfield's recipient of the Victoria Cross. William Coffey, another Irishman born in Knocklong, served with distinction in the Crimean War as a private in the 34th Foot (Border Regiment) where he won the French *Médaille militaire* as well as the VC for his heroism. He went on to fight at Lucknow during the Indian Mutiny and took up residence in Chesterfield after his discharge. William Coffey was still only in his forties when he died in 1875, and for many years his grave remained unmarked. Fortunately this sad state of affairs was put right in 1970, when his old regiment raised the funds for a headstone, and the grave was blessed at a ceremony attended by twenty old soldiers and the President of the Border Regiment Association on 19 September.

These are just a few of the figures who enlivened Victorian Chesterfield, and in their different ways each of them made his mark. George Stephenson may be the best known of Chesterfield's Victorians, but he was not alone in merit.

CHAPTER 12

Modern Times:
the Twentieth Century

The period 1892 to 1939 saw the emergence of Chesterfield as a prosperous, thriving and pleasant town in which its inhabitants could take a well-deserved pride. Much remained for the council of the newly extended borough to tackle, but tackle it they did, and with great success. The next thirty years saw continued advances on all possible fronts. Further extensions brought most of Hasland inside the borough boundary by 1910, and in 1920 Newbold and the three districts of Whittington were admitted to the fold. Home to some 13,000 people before 1892, by 1911 Chesterfield had a population of 37,406 and, by 1921, of 61,232! The increase in acreage was even greater, the original 322 grown to 2,643 by 1911 and by 1921 to 8,474. Increased by more than twenty times its original size, and with a far larger population, the town now had the financial and industrial muscle, as well as the political will, to take on the problems that had plagued it for so long.

First and most important was the issue of public health, and the grim decaying yards in the centre of the town. Charles P. Markham, now a council member and later to be mayor, clearly regarded them as an eyesore and a health hazard, a view shared by his sister Violet. Markham contributed generously to the cause, and when the work began to clear away the slum housing of the Dog Kennels and the worst of the yards and courts off Low Pavement, a grateful council named the new thoroughfare that replaced part of the area as Markham Road. By the late 1920s, the central slums of Chesterfield had disappeared, with a modern town rising from the wreckage.

A leading local industrialist, C.P. Markham, built good houses for his workers at the Broad Oaks engineering works on Piccadilly Road. In Brampton the Robinsons, always concerned with the well-

George MacMahon, pictured in the library at the Stephenson Memorial Hall. Born in Chesterfield to Irish immigrant parents, he succeeded fellow Irishman and staunch Roman Catholic Dennis Gorman in the post of librarian in 1909 and was in office when he died in 1921.

Stephenson Memorial Hall. Opened by the Duke of Devonshire on 14 July 1879, the hall was devised as a tribute to George Stephenson and a venue for educational activities. Later the public library, it is now the home of Chesterfield Museum and the Pomegranate Theatre.

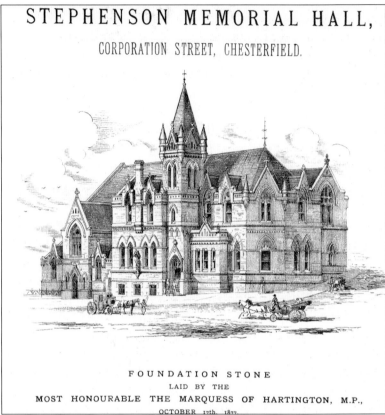

STEPHENSON MEMORIAL HALL,

CORPORATION STREET, CHESTERFIELD.

FOUNDATION STONE
LAID BY THE
MOST HONOURABLE THE MARQUESS OF HARTINGTON, M.P.,
OCTOBER 17th, 1877.

being of their employees, built the Wheatbridge estate, and established sporting, leisure and welfare facilities. Other public health amenities followed – the Slipper Baths on South Place in 1904, the Corporation Abattoir in 1933. By then, Chesterfield was a far healthier and more attractive place than in 1892.

For the first time, heavy industry appeared inside the borough. Markham, who had succeeded his father on the board of the Staveley Company and was to become its chairman in 1903, bought the Broad Oaks foundry site previously occupied by the Oliver family and established Markham & Co. Ltd in 1889. Situated at the eastern edge of the town close to the foot of Hady Hill, this engineering firm produced colliery winding gear, blast furnaces and other equipment geared to the thriving network of collieries that had been sunk in eastern Derbyshire, Nottinghamshire and South Yorkshire at the turn of the century, many of them operated by Markham's Staveley Company and its local rival the Sheepbridge Coal & Iron Company. Bryan Donkin Ltd arrived later, in 1903, sharing their Derby Road site with Clench & Co. before taking them over. Donkin produced equipment for the gas industry. On the far side of the town, on the corner of Brewery Street and Infirmary Road, the Chesterfield Tube Co. Ltd supplied gas cylinders and tubes for railway locomotives and boilers. To the west, Brampton was represented by the Plowright Brothers engineering firm, whose products were again used mainly by the collieries of Derbyshire and the outlying counties, and by J.B. Robinson & Son with their packaging and surgical dressings. These firms brought wealth and success to their owners, and to the town where they were based. Like most businesses of the time, they tended to adopt a paternalistic line with workers, setting up welfare and sporting facilities for them, but discouraging any trade union involvement. Away from the factories, in the mines and on the railways, there was strong union participation, and the local miners' representatives, James Haslam and William E. Harvey, were household names. Proof of the claim that British Socialism owed more to Methodism than to Marx, both men were lay preachers who won admiration for their moderation and restraint during the disputes of the 1890s. James Haslam was elected miners' MP for Chesterfield, and his friend Harvey represented North East Derbyshire. When they died within a year of each other, Haslam in 1913, and Harvey in 1914, both were honoured with statues outside the union offices on Saltergate. The NUM no longer occupies the office building, but the statues – both officially listed – remain standing.

Heavy industry brought numerous benefits to Chesterfield, but the Market Place retained its position as the centre for town life. It was greatly improved by the building of the new cattle market off Wheeldon Lane in 1900, which did away with the scenes recalled by Pendleton and

Charles Paxton Markham. The son of industrialist Charles Markham, C.P. Markham succeeded his father as head of the Staveley Coal & Iron Company, where he pioneered chemical production, and was also founder of the Broad Oaks Foundry (Markham Engineering) in Chesterfield itself. Three times mayor, he contributed to hospital and housing schemes, notably the Markham Road development and the demolition of the central slums. He bequeathed Tapton House and park to the town in 1925, a year before his death.

Chesterfield's electric tramway. Labourers at work on the line in Cavendish Street in 1904.

Trial run for the electric tram car, 3 December 1904.

Jacques in *Modern Chesterfield*. It also profited from advances in transport. The horse-drawn trams of 1882 gave way in 1904 to the new electric tramway that ran from Low Pavement to the Terminus Hotel in Brampton, and north from the town to Whittington Moor, allowing quick and easy travel to and from the Market Place itself. The North Midland Railway (now the Midland) was joined at the turn of the century by two more lines, the Great Central 'Chesterfield Loop' passing through a tunnel beneath Hollis Lane to emerge at its station on Infirmary Road, while the Lancashire, Derbyshire & East Coast Railway came through from Arkwright Town to halt at a third 'Market Place' station on the corner of Low Pavement near the Portland Hotel. As in the earliest days, all roads led to Chesterfield, and the same was true for the trains and the trams! The 1890s saw the water supply vastly improved, while in the early 1900s increased gas consumption for household appliances was matched by the return of electricity with a generating station established in the town.

Away from the Market Place, trade revolved around the shops and stores in the town centre. The twentieth century saw the start of one important career when Meshe David Osinsky, a Jewish

After Robinson's, the largest Brampton firm was Plowright Engineering, which employed local men for half a century until closure in the 1950s. The firm made equipment for local collieries, and this wartime picture shows Jesse Lilley (right, foreground) who later became a school attendance officer. He was the father of recently retired Local Studies Librarian John Lilley.

immigrant from Lithuania, opened his shop in Holywell Street in 1911. When he left, it was to make his name worldwide as Montagu Burton, 'the tailor of taste'. It has been claimed that Michael Marks, founder of Marks & Spencer, had a stall on the market, but this has yet to be confirmed. The Shopping Festivals of 1910 and 1914 paid tribute to the

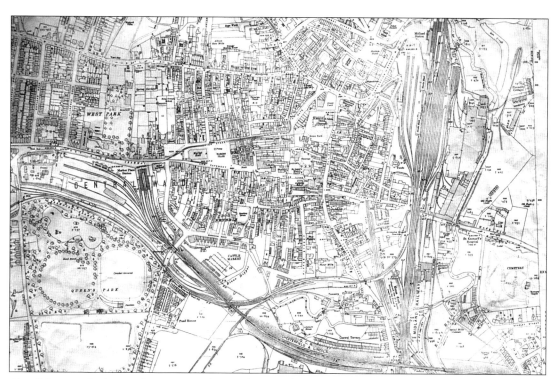

Detail from an Ordnance Survey map of 1918 showing the town centre and the network of communications linking Chesterfield with neighbouring districts. At this time the town boasted three railways and electric tramway services to Brampton and Whittington Moor.

Funeral of 'Picture Palace' victims, January 1912. In December 1911 a fire broke out in the cinema's dressing-room where several young girls were preparing to take part in a Christmas pantomime. Five of them perished in the ensuing blaze.

long-established Chesterfield firms like furniture makers Eyre & Sons, and the outfitter John Turner. Later these would be joined by international names such as Woolworth and Marks & Spencer.

Great strides were made in educational provision, a programme of school building in the 1900s followed by the first efforts at further education with the after-hours use of the grammar school for a number of courses. Later on, Alderman G. A. Eastwood presented the council with a site on Infirmary Road, on which the Chesterfield Technical College was built, opening to students in 1924. Most impressive of all was the three-year programme for primary and secondary education set out by Chesterfield in response to a new drive by the Board of Education, who offered a greatly increased grant on capital expenditure. Spearheaded by the redoubtable Violet Markham, and ably supported by such local worthies as Sir Ernest Shentall, W.H. Edmunds and Harry Cropper, the scheme totally restructured education in the town, closing three old schools, adapting three more to modern use, and erecting three new school buildings. Completed by 1932, the programme and its success is described in detail in *Chesterfield Education*, published in the same year. It was, and remains, a magnificent achievement.

Reconstruction was the order of the day, in every sense. New housing was built in the borough and existing stock improved, with the addition of more modern household facilities and appliances. The council moved out from their rooms in the Stephenson Memorial Hall to a new purpose-built town hall on Rose Hill in 1938, and the public library took over the vacated space. Following an adverse report from Sheffield's chief librarian, R.H. Gordon, the service had made the change from closed to open access, helped by a grant from the Carnegie United Kingdom Trust and even more by the exceptional talents of the librarian, W.H. Smettem. Smettem totally reorganized the library service in Chesterfield, and the work was carried on by his successor L.C. Jackson, with the first children's library opening in 1936 (one of the speakers was 'Grey Owl', since celebrated on cinema screens) and new extensions due to be officially opened in 1939. Unfortunately, the outbreak of the Second World War put a stop to this.

It was not 'all work and no play' in Chesterfield. T.P. Wood's lead with Queen's Park was followed by Alderman G.A. Eastwood (also a resident at Brambling House), who presented Eastwood Park to the people of Hasland in 1911, while Brearley Park was established in the Whittington area. A night at the theatre, or the cinema, was an option taken by many, and there were plenty to choose from. The Corporation Theatre and the Hippodrome on Corporation Street were rivalled by the Palace cinema on Burlington Street and the Odeon on Stephenson Place, while Brampton had its Coliseum on

Chatsworth Road and Whittington Moor its Lyceum, where for a time a youthful Joe Davis stood in as projectionist before becoming a snooker star. Dance venues abounded, notably the Victoria Ballroom, and St James Hall on Vicar Lane, and the converted malt warehouse on Sheffield Road known as the Rendezvous, once a magnet for dancers from all over the East Midlands but now sadly vanished. Sports fans could attend the cricket matches at Queen's Park or watch their soccer heroes at Saltergate, where the pre-war Chesterfield side fought its way into Division Two. Then again, they might prefer to skate at the West Bars rink, or watch the roller hockey matches or the boxing and wrestling bouts that took place at the Rendezvous in the late 1930s. The town had annual fairs, and regular visits from circuses and travelling shows. Buffalo Bill Cody's Wild West Show was in town for the day in 1903, although the event is thinly documented. Circuses such as Bertram Mills' usually occupied the open fields off Derby Road, often parading their animals up Corporation Street into town, and on one occasion in the 1900s the town enjoyed an unscheduled elephant stampede. Locals also enjoyed home-made entertainment with annual carnivals and music festivals, and the Empire Day celebrations that always featured strongly in the pre-war calendar.

As with every age, death and tragedy were never absent from the scene, and if we only wanted to hear the bad news, the first half of the twentieth century in Chesterfield could easily be presented as a catalogue of misery and disaster. Chesterfield men fought and died in the Boer War, or returned with crippling wounds, a foretaste of the far more widespread and appalling loss of life that would take place after 1914. Like other towns throughout the country, Chesterfield sent its young men to perish and be maimed in the cauldron of the First World War, and its Sherwood Foresters Regiment suffered heavy losses in the trench battles of the Somme and Passchendaele. The butchery of so many youngsters was a terrible blow, and the names on the war memorials in the Chesterfield districts tell their own grim story. The war had barely ended when the town was hit by the murderous flu epidemic that decimated populations around the world, and claimed even more victims than that terrible conflict had done. In three weeks in November 1918 Chesterfield saw over 100 burials in the Spital and Brampton St Thomas cemeteries, some of them young servicemen returning home and thinking their troubles were finally over! The years between the wars saw the General Strike of 1926, a rather grand name for a dispute that involved the whole trade

Picture House, Holywell Street, in 1936. Opened in 1923, the cinema was later renamed the Odeon. Among its regular organists was Edwin Booth, who taught the famous Reg Dixon at the cinema organ. Closed in 1981, the building is now the Winding Wheel Conference Centre.

Elephants from Bertram Mills' Circus in procession along Corporation Street in 1953.

Town hall, Rose Hill. Designed by architect A.J. Hope and built by Robert Carlyle & Co. Ltd, the town hall was opened on 6 April 1938 by the Duchess of Devonshire. The building, in the Georgian style, was described as being 'of austere character, with interesting mass and restrained colour.'

union movement for only a month, and where most of the suffering was endured by the miners and their families, who held out vainly for over a year only to be forced back for longer hours and lower wages. The 1930s had the Depression, with the town providing accommodation for the Unemployed Workers and the Jarrow Marchers on their way to register their protest in London. In the end, the unemployment problem was solved only by war in 1939.

1911 was an eventful year in Chesterfield, for all the wrong reasons. A railway strike in August led to disruption and the threat of violence, and the town's magistrates decided to close all public houses on the Saturday night of 19 August in order to avoid trouble. A better recipe for discontent is hard to imagine, but then hindsight is a wonderful thing. In the event a 600-strong crowd gathered outside the Midland Railway station at 9p.m., where railway staff and passengers were besieged inside the building. Police coming to the scene were greeted with a hail of missiles, and a series of baton charges ended with the constables retreating down Corporation Street 'in as good order as possible' under fire as the mob grew in size and strength. This went on until 1a.m., when a unit of soldiers arrived from their camp at Barrow Hill. The police still having made no headway, Mayor Charles P. Markham arrived and read the Riot Act as missiles still flew through the air. The troops charged up Corporation Street with fixed bayonets, and the rioters fled, but regrouped around St Mary's Gate and Holywell Street. After further police charges and what amounted to a running battle through the centre of town, the crowd dispersed and prisoners were taken. The riot, which lasted for over four hours, is still by far the worst disturbance in Chesterfield's history. One can easily imagine what a feast it would make for television reporters in our own time. It also gives the lie to those who would have us believe that 'we didn't have violence in those days'!

December of the same year saw the terrible fire at the Picture Palace on Burlington Street, when a spark from the fire in a dressing-room ignited the dresses of a group of young girls waiting to perform an Eskimo scene in a Christmas pantomime. Five girls died from the severe burns they suffered, and although the cinema has long since disappeared their ghosts are said to haunt the site.

Then, as always, Chesterfield had no shortage of bad news to report, but in spite of all the horrors they endured its people generally enjoyed a better standard of life than their Victorian ancestors. In terms of housing, education, leisure, wages and labour-saving devices, life in the town had advanced from the grim days of the 1890s and before. Even the new horror of Hitler and his global threat to peace could not set it back. Chesterfield endured the Second World War without lasting damage. There was a blackout, as there had been in the previous war, and defensive preparations were made with sandbags protecting the town hall, the establishing of air-raid shelters, and regular fire-watching duties for local government personnel. Bombs fell on factory sites and outlying villages, but fortunately the town did not suffer as Sheffield did in December 1940. The war memorials remind us of Chesterfield men and women who fought and did not return, but their town remained unscathed.

Victory had been won, but at a cost and further dramatic changes lay ahead. The world that had been before the war had gone, and would not return.

William Home Smettem, who became Chesterfield's librarian in 1926. A man of exceptional ability, he transformed the service in his three years of office, making the change to open access, establishing high standards and setting up extra-mural classes before leaving to do the same for Scarborough in 1929.

Wartime amphibious landing craft loaded for delivery at Markham Engineering Works, in the yard outside the drawing office. The firm made thirty-one of these for military use during the Second World War. The man in the suit is Dennis Revill, and to his left is Arthur Large.

CHAPTER 13

When the War was Over: 1950-2000

Britain had gone to war in 1939 as an imperial power. She came out of it with that power greatly reduced, and with former colonies and dominions demanding their independence. Standing alone against Hitler's onslaught for eighteen months and more, her people had shown great heroism and endurance, but the strain had told, and the post-war era saw Britain overshadowed by the superpower struggle between America and the Soviet Union which would continue into the 1990s. Like it or not, Britain was no longer a 'great power' able to impose her will on the world.

Chesterfield saw sweeping changes in the second half of the century. An obvious example was the decline of manufacturing industry in the town. The writing was on the wall with the demise of the formerly lucrative breweries. The Chesterfield Brewery was first to cease operations, taken over by the Mansfield Brewery in 1934. The following year George Kenning, head of the Clay Cross motor engineering firm, bought the buildings, later selling them to Trebor the sweet manufacturer. The 1950s saw the end of the other two. Walker & Richardson of Newark took over the Brampton Brewery in 1955, and the last Brampton ale was brewed on 15 June. Following further takeovers by John Smith and Courage, the buildings were finally demolished in 1984, and the site is now occupied by a B&Q store. The Scarsdale Brewery, taken over by Whitbread in 1958, ceased brewing a year later. The brewery was destroyed in 1961, although the office – a listed building – is still in use.

After the breweries, it was the turn of the railways. The Market Place Station ceased running passenger services in 1951, and by the '60s freight deliveries had also halted. The Great Central Station and its line fell into disuse in the 1960s, victims of Dr Beeching's ill-fated drive to shift transport from rail to road. Nowadays a barred gate blocks the Hollis Lane tunnel, and stations and lines are no more than a memory. Only the former Midland Station, greatly altered, continues in service.

Chesterfield at war: a German mine on display in the centre of town.

Goods van No. 64336 enters the Market Place Station in January 1952. On the right is the Portland Hotel, while the town hall is shown in the background to the left.

Newland Gardens, Newbold. This 1947 photograph by Fred Jacques shows Chesterfield's post-war housing at its most idyllic.

The 1951 Festival of Britain celebrations must have seemed to many to be ushering in a bright new era, and the 1960s and '70s still offered some cause for optimism. The Market Place Station's demolition, for example, made way for the arrival of the Accountant General's Department on West Bars, which was opened in 1962, complete with its controversial Barbara Hepworth sculpture. The AGD, as this large administrative office block for postal service employees came to be known, provided jobs for a large number of Chesterfield people for nearly forty years, and became a distinctive local landmark. Its own time came in 1989, when it too was demolished to make way for a new Post Office building, Rowland Hill House.

In 1974 Chesterfield Borough made its most recent extension, taking in the outlying districts of Staveley, Brimington and Inkersall, and once more greatly increasing its area and population. Once again, the future of the town seemed bright.

By the 1980s the stormclouds had returned. The decline of the coal industry and the loss of railway traffic deprived Chesterfield's factories of vital markets for their goods. The Staveley

Company, which had diversified into chemical products before the First World War, pursued this line of research and production in later years. It was taken over by the French corporation Rhone-Poulenc in the 1990s. Markham, whose founder C.P. Markham died in 1926, developed tunnelling and other equipment for water companies around the world, and in their last decade produced giant earth-boring engines for work on the Channel Tunnel. Sadly none of these innovations were enough to save the firm, and shortly after being taken over by the Swedish company Kvaerner the factory was closed in 1997, after almost a century in existence. Reduced production, short-time working and redundancies threatened Donkin and Sterling Tubes, the town's other engineering firms, and the Whittington company Dema Glass. As the twentieth century, and the Millennium, came to an end, Chesterfield's future appeared increasingly to lie with the long-established service industries, and with information technology, leisure and tourism. The town would need to reinvent itself to meet the challenge of the twenty-first century.

Markham Engineering Works, Hollis Lane, viewed from Clayton Street in late 2000, three years after the firm ceased operations in 1997.

Giant tunnelling machine for work on the Channel Tunnel, pictured at Markham Engineering Works in 1988. Sadly, such innovations could not save the firm from closure.

CHAPTER 14

Names to Conjure With:
A Few Twentieth Century Celebrities

As in previous centuries, the past hundred years saw Chesterfield linked with several notable personalities, a handful of whom now come in for mention.

Sir Robert Robinson has to be the most eminent of all modern Cestrefeldians. Grandson of John Bradbury Robinson, who founded the Brampton packaging firm in 1839, he was born at Rufford House on Baslow Road in 1886, and educated at Chesterfield Grammar School before graduating with First Class Honours as a BSc from Manchester University. He went on to establish himself as one of the leading research chemists of his time, winning a staggering number of university professorships and academic awards. Knighted in 1939, he received the Nobel Prize for Chemistry in 1947, the Albert Medal as 'the greatest organic chemist of our time' in the same year, was a member and later president of the Royal Society, and in 1949 was awarded the Order of Merit (given only to twenty-five recipients during their lifetime). A research consultant for ICI and a director of the family firm, he was made a Freeman of his native town of Chesterfield in 1947, his Nobel Prize-winning year. A man of many talents, Sir Robert was not only an eminent chemist but an expert photographer and mountain climber and an

Sir Robert Robinson. A member of the well-known Brampton industrial family, Sir Robert was knighted in 1939, and in 1947 awarded the Nobel Prize for Chemistry, together with the prestigious Albert Medal as 'the greatest organic chemist of our time.' A Companion of Honour, he is buried in Westminster Abbey. (Picture courtesy of Robinson & Sons)

Fair on Holywell Street car park, August Bank Holiday weekend 1987. (Copyright Derbyshire Times)

Rufford House, Baslow Road, birthplace of Sir Robert Robinson. (Picture courtesy of Robinson & Sons)

exceptional chess player. Twice Oxford champion in the 1930s, he was apparently able to play twenty-four games simultaneously, winning twenty-two and stalemating the others! When he died in 1975, he was honoured with a service in Westminster Abbey.

Aviation pioneers, the Short brothers, who originated from further south, lived for a time in the Whittington area. Horace Short and a companion made a balloon ascent from Queen's Park on 2 August 1905. His brother Eustace was one of the first Britons to fly with the Wright brothers, and Shorts later produced Wright aircraft in the UK. Members of the family later established the firm of Short Brothers in Belfast, where the Stirling bomber and Sunderland flying boat were manufactured.

The Sheffield stainless steel pioneer Harry Brearley lived in Walton, a western district of Chesterfield, during the 1930s. By then his discoveries had already been honoured by the town, with his name being given to Brearley Park in New Whittington.

Sir Harry Lauder, the great Scottish entertainer, had a brief but definite Chesterfield connection. The family lived for a year at Whittington Moor when his father John worked for Pearson's Pottery, but moved away following John Lauder's untimely death. Sir Harry came back on two occasions to visit the town, the first in 1915 when he toured with an army recruiting band, and later in 1948 to visit his father's grave in Newbold churchyard.

Novelist and poet Frederick Charles Boden was born in Matlock but grew up as a child and young man in the centre of Chesterfield. The town provides the setting for most of his works. *Miner*, the best known of his novels, depicts a memorable and harrowing picture of mining life, culminating in the 1926 strike and its aftermath. *Flo* and *A Derbyshire Tragedy* are almost as impressive, the former with its racy theme of a young man's involvement with two different women rather daring for the 1930s. His poems, many with Chesterfield settings, are contained in two collections, *Pithead Poems* and *Out of the Coalfields*. Boden, whose work was also broadcast on radio, was hailed as a new discovery in pre-war days, but his writing has since tended to be overlooked. This is a pity, as his books are worth reading both for themselves and for their insight into life in and around Chesterfield in the 1920s and '30s.

Harry Brearley, the famous Sheffield stainless steel pioneer, pictured with his wife at their home in Walton during the 1930s.

Captain Percy Sillitoe served as Chesterfield's Chief Constable from 1923 to 1925 before leaving to become even more famous as the 'gang-busting' Chief Constable of Sheffield, where he has been credited with the restoration of law and order to the city. In later years he became the head of MI5, and received a knighthood for his services.

There are other Cestrefeldians who, while perhaps not household names, ought to be far better known. An excellent example is Oliver

Bob Wilson at Saltergate, 1991. Born in Chesterfield to Scottish parents, Bob Wilson was the first English-born player to be chosen as a Scottish international, and starred as Arsenal goalkeeper in their FA Cup and League 'double' year of 1971. Nowadays better known as a popular TV personality, he is pictured here with Jack Hemmings and manager Chris McMenemy. (Copyright Derbyshire Times)

Smalley, born in the town where his father was licensee of the Nag's Head, and educated at Chesterfield Grammar School where he captained the school football team. After working with Armstrong Whitworth as director of research and development, Oliver went to the USA in 1925, making his name as an expert in the manufacture of electric steel and the production of steel from iron ore. One of the world's leading metal experts, he rose to President of the Meehanite Metal Corporation in New Rochelle, was appointed a member of the Advisory Council for Science and Engineering at the University of Notre Dame, USA, and served for fifteen years as British Consul. During the Second World War he raised $3.5 million dollars for wartime charities, and was rewarded with an OBE from King George VI during a royal visit to the United States. His is surely a success story of which fellow Cestrefeldians should be proud.

Equally deserving of recognition is the late W. Horace Barnett, founder of Chesterfield's own astronomical observatory. Born in Chesterfield, Horace left school early to work at Markham Colliery and the Chesterfield Tube Works before serving in the army during the Second World War. A founder member of the Chesterfield Astronomical Society, he was responsible for setting up the Barnett Observatory on Hastings Close in Newbold. Almost entirely self-educated, Horace Barnett demonstrated an astonishing range of talents; with the help of a handful of equally gifted colleagues he designed the telescope and supervised its construction and installation in the 18-foot hemispherical dome, where six supporting rollers and a further six side rollers allowed finger-tip movement through 360 degrees. The observatory was opened in 1960 by the Astronomer Royal, Dr R. van der Riet Woolley, who described it as 'the best observatory owned by any amateur society in the country'. A great success for almost forty years, the observatory was briefly threatened with closure when the society was presented with a sharp increase in rental payments, but thanks to the support of the public and the personal intervention of astronomer Patrick Moore, the crisis was averted. Horace Barnett died in 1999 at the age of eighty-two, but the newly equipped and renovated observatory continues to thrive and to draw large numbers of visitors. All the more reason for its native-born designer to receive the honour which is no more than his due.

Bob Wilson has for several years been a popular television personality and sports commentator, whose Chesterfield origins are well known. Born in the town, Bob was the son of Scottish parents, his father W.S. Wilson serving as Borough Surveyor. Educated at Chesterfield Grammar School, Bob played football for England Schoolboys before going on to make his career as a goalkeeper in the top flight. A member of the Arsenal side that won the European Fairs Cup in 1970, and the 'double' of League and F.A. Cup in 1971, he was also the first English-born Scottish international. Since retiring from the game, he became a familiar face on the TV screen as a long-serving commentator and presenter for BBC's *Grandstand* and *Football Focus* programmes, before moving to join ITV as presenter for the midweek *Big Match* in 1994. Bob, who watched Chesterfield play at Saltergate as a boy, has often returned to his home town, and took a keen interest in the Spireites' FA Cup run of 1997. He is probably the best-known Chesterfield 'face' of modern times.

Thanks to his achievements, and those of the others mentioned here, the name of Chesterfield has been brought before a wider public around the world.

CHAPTER 15

What About the Women? Chesterfield 'Herstory'

Until very recently, the study of history has tended to be exactly that; 'his story'. The nature and extent of the female contribution to our heritage has all too often been overlooked. This is as true of Chesterfield as anywhere else, and the following is a small attempt to redress the balance.

For most of the period covered by this book, Chesterfield's women were denied the rights enjoyed by men. Unable to vote until the 1920s, for the most part they did not own property and were imprisoned within an endless sequence of domestic duties, not least bearing children, which could all too often be the cause of a woman's death. Worst of all, they were subjected to brutal and degrading punishments not handed out to the men. Women who had the temerity to speak up for themselves were 'scolds', and could expect to be immersed on the ducking-stool kept at the water's edge by the Silk Mill dam. If this was an unpleasant experience, even worse was the 'brank' or 'scold's bridle', a close-fitting metal cage that covered the head and held the tongue fast with a jagged iron bit. Both these punishments were apparently continued until early in the eighteenth century, and are a shameful reminder of the way half the town's population could expect to be treated.

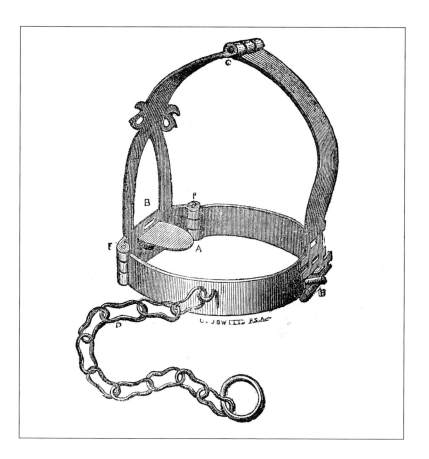

The 'brank' or 'scold's bridle', a vicious punishment meted out to Chesterfield women up until the eighteenth century, and a shameful reminder of past brutalities.

A suffragette addresses a largely male audience in Chesterfield Market Place, some time between 1910 and 1914. The shops of Low Pavement are visible in the background.

Even in those early days, some spirited females were making their own way in the world. Widows came into the property of their husbands, and often showed a talent for business. In the year 1185 one of the Chesterfield tenants of the Knights Templars was the unnamed widow of Richard the tanner, who had evidently inherited his tenancy. Rather less edifying is a reference to 'Mary Clarke, fornicatrix', who obviously made a living in the 'oldest profession'! Medieval Chesterfield also had its first female royal visit, when Eleanor, wife of Edward I, journeyed through the town in the year 1290. By Tudor times some ladies were beginning to adapt to the rules of a male-rigged game. Bess of Hardwick, whose henpecked consort, the Earl of Shrewsbury, was lord of the manor to Chesterfield, rose to wealth and fame by a well-judged series of marriages to rich, and mostly short-lived husbands. No doubt there were others who adopted similar methods at a lower level of society. These, though, were exceptions that proved the rule. Male attitudes dominated, and even Queen Elizabeth I for much of her reign was obliged to act a part that suited the prejudices of court and nation.

Female munitions workers at the Patent Electric Shot-firing Company during the First World War. Based at Dark Lane, Newbold, the firm made detonators for the coal industry in peacetime, and during the war produced the filling for hand grenades or 'Mills bombs'. The factory closed in 1957.

A ladies' football team made up of Robinsons' employees, some time between 1910 and 1920. Contrary to what many people think, ladies' teams were widespread before the Second World War, and are now making a comeback.

There was, it seemed, no substitute for money. Private incomes, whether inherited or acquired, allowed more freedom to the lucky few, not least the liberty to travel. Visitors like Celia Fiennes in 1697 and Anna Seward, the poetess 'Swan of Lichfield', are good examples. From what we know of the town at that time, Chesterfield had no-one to match their good fortune.

The drive for female emancipation gathered momentum with the suffragette movement, begun in late Victorian times and continued up to the First World War. Mrs Emmeline Pankhurst, the formidable Wythenshawe registrar, was its best-known figure, but the movement had several 'stars' and like most nationwide organizations soon divided into 'moderate' and 'radical' wings. The 'moderates', represented by the National Union of Women's Suffrage Societies, evidently gained a strong following among middle-class families in Chesterfield. When George MacMahon, Chesterfield's librarian, received a letter from the local branch of the society in 1914, requesting that their journal *The Common Cause* be made available in the library, the letter was accompanied by a petition whose signatories included the names of some well-known Chesterfield families. Not too surprisingly, the library committee agreed to take the journal. The suffragettes held at least one public meeting in Chesterfield Market Place, and in 1914 the parish church was closed due to fear of vandalism, several other places of worship having been fired by the more radical members of the sisterhood. Perhaps most interesting is Chesterfield's own contribution to the movement abroad. Emma Holmes, born to a family in Packers Row in 1839, and who later lived on Saltergate, left Chesterfield and Britain to win fame as Emma Miller in Australia, where, as a prominent member of the suffragette movement and the Labour Party, and a pioneer of female trade unions, she played an important part in securing the federal vote for Australian women in 1902. Honoured in her adopted country ever since her death in 1917, her fame has only recently filtered back to her native town.

The First World War gave further impetus to women's rights. With the men fighting at the front, it was women who kept the war effort going at home. They drove the Chesterfield trams, now increasingly a danger as track and vehicles began to show signs of wear and tear. They toiled in the munitions factories, like that of the Patent Electric Shot-Firing Company on Dark Lane in Newbold, where they made fuses and detonators for the hand-grenades known as 'Mills bombs'. When the war ended and the clamour for equal voting rights began, it was no longer so easy to hold back the tide. When the right to vote was finally won, it came none too soon, and was the result of many personal sacrifices by women in Chesterfield and elsewhere.

There were rare individual success stories, of course. Olave St Clair Soames, born at Stubbing Court in Wingerworth, was daughter of the owner of the Brampton Brewery. Part of her childhood was spent in Chesterfield, in West House on West Bars, but she had left the town by the time she married Robert Baden Powell and became an international figure as head of the Girl Guide movement. Katherine Bacon, whose father operated the firm of Cavendish Motors on Holywell Street, achieved teenage stardom as a concert pianist, performing in public at the Market Hall when only thirteen years old. Married at nineteen to tutor and fellow pianist Arthur Newstead, she emigrated to America where stardom continued. Katherine played at Carnegie Hall with the New York Philharmonic Orchestra to great acclaim, and in 1925 visited Britain for performances at the Wigmore Hall as well as in her native Chesterfield.

No individual, male or female, is more deserving of praise than Violet Markham. Born to a privileged upbringing as the child of industrialist Charles Markham and his wife Rosa Paxton, whose father Sir Joseph Paxton designed the Crystal Palace, she and her brothers Charles P. Markham and Sir Arthur B. Markham, MP, all achieved prominence in public life. More than her siblings, Violet was to campaign vigorously to better the lot of those less fortunate than herself, supporting a mass of public health, welfare, youth and educational issues. Made independent by a legacy in 1901, she flung herself with great energy into a career of public service. First female member of Chesterfield's School Board where she was a key figure for nearly forty years, and first woman on the Borough Council, she coerced her colleagues into increasing education budgets and was at the forefront of the school reorganization drive of 1929-32. Appalled by the filthy state of the town, and the degraded lives of many of its inhabitants, in 1902 she put her own money into founding the Chesterfield Settlement, a pioneering body that provided mother and baby clinics, youth and outreach activities, and further education, long before many of these were available through the formal channels. The settlement closed in 1957, by which time Violet had long since won national and international fame. Chairman of the Central Committee on Women's Training and Employment, and Deputy Director of the National Relief Fund in the First World War, in 1923 she represented the Canadian government on the governing body of the International Labour Office in Geneva. A woman of tremendous vision, she was also extremely practical, setting up and running a canteen in the Second World War, and re-starting it from new premises when it was bombed.

Margaret Whitmore. A district midwife from 1918 to the 1930s, she typifies the many unsung heroines who performed a vital service to the community without winning celebrity status.

Violet Markham in her mayoral year of 1927-28. The first woman to hold the office, and Chesterfield's first female Freeman in 1954, she was a dynamic and visionary pioneer in local education, health and welfare, and a key figure in the making of modern Chesterfield.

In her own town she showed the same approach, campaigning for improved health care and a clean water supply, and pulling no punches in condemning the shortcomings of Chesterfield itself. Hers was a leading voice in the eventual 'cleaning-up' of the old Victorian borough, and it was only fitting that Chesterfield should honour her as its first woman mayor in 1927 and first female Freeman in 1954. A talented public speaker and tireless worker, Violet was also a prolific author, with several books to her name. Of these, *Paxton and the Bachelor Duke* details the story of her grandfather, the head gardener of Chatsworth, while in *Transformation of a Town* she gives a tough and thought-provoking account of Chesterfield's emergence from the slum era of the old borough. Her own story is told in *Return Passage*, and *Friendship's Harvest* recalls several notable acquaintances with affection and humour. Chesterfield owes much to this magnificent woman, whose life was spent in improving the lot of others. When she died in 1959 in her ninety-first year, she was mourned by the town she had served so well. Her example created a precedent for others to follow, and Blanche Eastwood and Florence Robinson were two others who served ably after her in the government of the town.

These women, and others not mentioned here, helped to win the freedoms enjoyed by their sisters today. Our own time has seen a rapturous welcome for a visiting princess, when Prince Charles and the late lamented Princess Diana came to Chesterfield to open the Pavements Shopping Centre in 1981. The love and affection the Princess inspired from the people of Chesterfield was evident to all, and has been strengthened even more by her tragic death. But today the historian need not rely on royal visits to mention the name of a famous woman, as was the case not so long ago. Nowadays women occupy leading roles in Chesterfield, as they do throughout the world. In Ann Ainsworth, the town has its first female chief librarian, and in Anne-Marie Knowles its first female museum curator, while in the world of business Glenys Goucher serves as Chief Executive for the North Derbyshire Chamber of Commerce. Perhaps even more significant is the fact that one in three of all new businesses created has a woman at its head. It is an impressive statistic.

A great deal more remains to be done, but for what has so far been achieved these pioneering sisters deserve to be remembered. They, and others like them, are part of a Chesterfield 'herstory' that is only now coming to light.

Chesterfield Shopping Festival advertisement for John Turner's outfitters on Packers Row and Vicar Lane in 1914. A large-scale enterprise which at one time employed an army of assistants, the business closed in the 1980s, and has since been replaced by the Pizza Hut.

CHAPTER 16

Infinite Diversity

Of all the ludicrous beliefs being aired nowadays, first prize surely has to go to the myth of 'racial purity.' Put bluntly, there ain't no such animal, and probably never was. Here in Britain, any chance of our being a 'pure' unmixed nation vanished around Roman times. And for the benefit of those unfamiliar with this country's history, people from Asia and Africa, as well as other parts of Europe, were here in Britain wearing Roman helmets long before any Anglo-Saxons arrived!

Chesterfield, of course, owes its name to a bunch of 'immigrants' from Italy (or maybe even farther afield) who called themselves the Romans. The men who built the settlement that later became the modern town may have hailed from that country, or Spain, or somewhere more exotic still. What is fairly certain is that the Roman soldiers had added to the gene pool of the native Coritani and Brigantes by the time they left a hundred years later.

The departure of the Romans left the gate open for the incoming Angles, who again were probably a mixture of peoples rather than a single separate nation. Within two hundred years they were themselves invaded by the Scandinavian Vikings, and we know that those who settled around Chesterfield included both Danes and Norwegians. Once again, interbreeding would most definitely have taken place as the different groups settled down together. Then in 1066 it was the turn of the

Swallows' outfitters, on the corner of Knifesmithgate and Packers Row. A well-established local business for many years, now a memory of times past.

Normans. The lords to whom William the Conqueror parcelled out the shires of England, and the retainers they brought with them, were the result of ethnic intermingling between Vikings and the French inhabitants of Normandy, and with *droit de seigneur* the order of the day Chesterfield folk would have seen yet another flavour added to the cultural melting pot.

Fortunately for her people, England was not successfully invaded again by a foreign power, but cultural mixing was far from over. Tudor and Stuart times saw the victims of religious persecution flee to England for their lives, and no doubt the influx of Flemish weavers, Dutch shoemakers and French Huguenot glassworkers left some trace in the Chesterfield area too. At least one black slave, a servant of the Jebb family in Georgian times, lies buried in Chesterfield today, and with the Napoleonic wars came the arrival of the French and Polish prisoners of war on parole in the town, several of whom married locally and at least one of whom stayed behind when the war was over. By the mid-nineteenth century a growing number of Irish workers and their families had chosen to make their homes in Chesterfield, and by doing so made a considerable contribution to the history of the town.

The twentieth century, so recently passed, has had its share of incoming groups and individuals. In its opening decades Chesterfield has been home to Jewish traders and entrepreneurs from Eastern Europe (Montagu Burton being the obvious example), German bandsmen, and Belgian refugees who stayed here during the First World War. The Second World War and the post-war decades have seen an even more varied inflow of peoples to the town and the surrounding area. Polish ex-servicemen, including paratroopers housed at the nearby Hardwick camp, came over to help fight the expected German invasion. They settled here when their country was seized by the Communists in 1945, as did former German and Italian prisoners of war, and Ukrainian and Hungarian refugees from Russian persecution in the 1940s and '50s.

The last fifty years have seen the arrival of other varied ethnic groups, all of whom have settled in the town and made their own valuable contribution to modern Chesterfield. They include individuals and families from Italy, from Greece and Cyprus, from southern China and Hong Kong, from the Caribbean islands, and the Indian subcontinent. Their story has as yet not been recorded, but is nevertheless a vital part of Chesterfield history, and the book is surely waiting to be written. With luck, the new Millennium will see the first efforts to record the memories of these 'new' inhabitants, some of whom have lived here for half a century by now, and whose experience is part of their town's unsung heritage. Chesterfield, like most places in the world, has always consisted of a blend of cultures and beliefs, all the richer for the diversity and the many different qualities contributed to the town. Like the Celts, Romans, Angles and Normans long ago, all are part of the whole, and can say with pride 'I am a Cestrefeldian.'

CHAPTER 17

A Note on the Weather

No English town's history would be complete without a brief comment on the weather, and Chesterfield has certainly had its share of freakish conditions over the past centuries. The torrential rain and heavy flooding that marked the year 2000 and has been attributed to global warming is exceptional, but past ages have experienced weather just as unusual.

The eighteenth century seems to have gone through a range of extremes. The winter and spring of 1778-79, for example, must have been one of the driest ever, with no rain or snow falling from 21 December to 25 April. The following spring kept up these Costa del Sol conditions, with cherry, plum and pear trees in full blossom by 25 March 1779. The 1790s were altogether less kind, 23 December 1790 brought a terrible storm to Chesterfield which caused damage to property in the town, setting the scene for a severe winter with storms of wind, hail, rain, thunder and lightning. Plenty of variety, if not of the kind most of us would like to encounter. Snow fell on 12 June 1791, and in 1795 the bad weather resulted in a severe grain shortage. The storms kept up throughout the decade, the winter of 1796-97 seeing constant high winds that badly damaged trees and buildings, while July and August 1799 were so wet that the corn crops suffered again.

The nineteenth century started with a bang, too. On 25 June 1830 'the most tremendous storm ever remembered' hit Chesterfield, doing severe damage to property and buildings. Two years later in 1832 it was the turn of heavy rain and floods. The Rother and Hipper had always been liable to flooding during rainy periods, which is probably why the former has the Celtic name of 'great river'. A fairly mild stream in pleasant weather, both it and its neighbour can become dangerous torrents when swollen by downpours, and so it proved in 1832. Both the Tapton and Spital bridges had to be rebuilt following structural damage by the floodwaters. Brampton and Spital, both low-lying areas in the vicinity of the rivers, usually suffered from flooding more than most. Two major floods swept through Brampton in the

Floodwater laps the windows of a house during the downpour of August Bank Holiday 1922, when 4 inches of rain left parts of Brampton submerged, and services were brought to a halt.

Chatsworth Road under a covering of snow following a heavy fall during the 1920s. This time, though, the weather did not prevent the trams from running.

Clayton Street underwater after heavy rain brought flooding to the town in November 2000.

Derby Road roundabout becomes a lake as the River Hipper bursts its banks to flood most of the main routes into town following the November 2000 downpour.

early twentieth century. The first, on August Bank Holiday Monday 1922, resulted from a sustained downpour that swelled the Hipper with 4 inches of rain. Chatsworth Road became a lake, houses were marooned in lagoons of water, transport was halted and businesses were unable to operate. The contemporary scene of a house with floodwater up to its windows sums up the misery of many locals on this worst of Bank Holidays! Ten years later, in 1932, the rains came down again, this time surpassing the previous fall with five inches of rain. Again Brampton was all but submerged, buses brought to a halt, and people rescued from flooded buildings. Robinsons' factory was badly flooded, looms damaged as the water rose three feet high in the weaving sheds and four feet high outside, and 800 workers had to be sent home.

Mid-century saw severe winters, notably that of 1947 when snow lay heavy on the ground from December into April, and the country was brought to a virtual standstill. Later 'freezes' in 1963 and 1979 were shorter-lived, but cold while they lasted; the sea froze in 1963, for instance, and 1990 saw north Derbyshire brought to a halt for a couple of weeks as snow and icy rain froze the power lines and put out lights in Chesterfield and the towns and villages around. On the other hand, the region experienced long hot summers in 1956 and 1976, though the latter was ushered in by a fierce June hailstorm that broke windows with stones the size of golf balls!

Floods have continued to plague Chesterfield in recent times. In 1987 heavy rain brought flooding to the area round Rhodesia Road, and to the junction of the A617 dual carriageway with Derby Road. The downpours of November 2000 saw spectacular flooding in Spital, with Clayton Street and the main road into town submerged in places, the Rother a raging torrent running past the disused Markham site, and huge lakes forming at Hollis Lane bridge, the Derby Road roundabout and the Inner Relief Road. Freak weather, one feels, is always going to be with us, perhaps more so today than in previous centuries. It's a nuisance, and sometimes a danger, but the general feeling is that 'Chesterfield can take it', if only because she doesn't have any other choice!

CHAPTER 18

New Millennium

As we enter the year 2001, Chesterfield once more stands on the brink of change. The engineering firms that were such an important factor in its growth – Markham & Co., Bryan Donkin Ltd, Sterling Tubes – have either already closed or are experiencing terminal difficulties, and the emphasis has switched to other types of industry.

Tourism is more central to Chesterfield's economy than ever before. The Peacock Inn on Low Pavement, a listed building dating from Tudor times, has since 1981 been restored for use as the Peacock Information & Heritage Centre, providing a valuable information service to new arrivals and

Wheatsheaf Inn, Newbold. A school in 1785, it was converted to a public house in 1863 and was one of 116 owned by the Brampton Brewery prior to takeover by Warwick & Richardsons of Newark in 1955.

Queen's Park Hotel, Park Road, 1994. This shows the attractively designed building and the row of housing running almost the length of Markham Road. Hotel and houses have since disappeared, the former replaced by Focus Do-it-All and the latter by the Ravenside Retail Park.

Red Lion, Vicar Lane, in 1987. For many years a fixture on Vicar Lane, this building was demolished in 1999 as part of the Vicar Lane retail development.

producing its own trails and tours to historic places in the town. Chesterfield's historic landmarks are secured by an active Civic Society, while the local Photographic Society with its five year rolling programme has ensured that any changes to areas and buildings in the town do not pass unnoticed. The Borough Museum, opened in 1994, is also a magnet for visitors. Housed in the Stephenson Memorial Hall on Corporation Street, where it shares premises with the Pomegranate Theatre in the old home of the Free Library, the museum preserves a wide range of artefacts and puts on regular exhibitions that bring aspects of Chesterfield's heritage to the attention of the visitor. The Pomegranate, formerly the Civic Theatre, has provided a lively diet of drama and entertainment ever since its opening in 1949. During that time it has helped to launch the careers of many famous actors and actresses, among them Margaret

Saint James' Hall, Vicar Lane. Built in 1894 by Revd Littleton in memory of his late mother, 'Jimmy's' was a popular venue for music and dancing in later years. Perhaps the most attractive building on Vicar Lane, it proved another casualty of the recent shopping development.

Tyzack, Penelope Keith, Peter Sallis, Bernard Archard and Sue Jenkins. One photograph of a Christmas pantomime in 1953 shows company regulars Nigel Davenport, Wilfred Brambell and David McCallum onstage together!

Leisure is a growing industry, and one that takes many forms. The popular venue of Queen's Park was in 1987 given a further valuable asset when the Queen's Park Leisure Centre was opened to the public. The centre provides health, fitness, sport and gymnasium facilities, with the large heated swimming pool a major attraction. The last thirty years have seen the closure of the cinemas in the centre of town. The Odeon has become the Winding Wheel conference centre, the ABC/Canon is no longer in use, and the site of the vanished Picture Palace is now inhabited by a Burger King restaurant. But away from the centre, off the Derby Road roundabout, the Alma Leisure Complex erected in the 1990s boasts a

No. 1 Bath Place, Lordsmill Street, in 1953. Described as the smallest house in Chesterfield, like much of the older housing in the town centre this building has now disappeared.

Hipper Corn Mill, viewed from Lordsmill Street in 1997, prior to demolition.

Bryan Donkin Engineering Works, seen from Lordsmill Street in 1997. One of the main engineering firms in the town, it has now ceased operations.

Falcon Yard. Once part of Chesterfield's urban decay, Falcon Yard and Low Pavement have since been restored and made attractive areas for locals and visitors alike, while retaining their historic character.

variety of facilities, among them Frankie & Benny's restaurant and the Cineworld multiplex cinema.

A far older leisure pursuit still popular today is 'going to the match'. Chesterfield Football Club still play their home games at Saltergate, the old Victorian 'Recreation Ground', although a new stadium remains a future possibility. The team that Bob Wilson watched as a lad has achieved much in recent years. Winning the Freight Rover trophy and promotion to Division Two was followed by heroic performances in the 1997 FA Cup run, where Chesterfield reached the semi-final against the Premiership's Middlesbrough. Most neutrals still feel they were robbed of victory in the first match which ended in a 2-2 draw, when what appeared to be a perfectly good Andy Morris goal was disallowed. Luck ran out in the replay, but the Spireites went out of the cup with their reputation intact, knowing they should have met Chelsea in the final. In the Cup, who knows what might have happened? And despite unfortunate events off the pitch, 2001 has seen the team secure promotion to Division Two with excellent performances on the field.

Information technology holds the key to future development, and Chesterfield has embraced the benefits of the computer age. Courses are available in the town at the College of Technology and Art on Infirmary Road, and the North Derbyshire Chamber of Commerce provides its own business-oriented courses at the Wharf Lane Training Centre. Chesterfield has several small firms specialising in computers, and a number of local website designers.

Service industries, always integral to a market town like Chesterfield, have if anything taken on greater importance in the 1980s and '90s. Disappearing manufacturing companies have given way to a wealth of supermarkets, DIY stores and major shopping developments. The Pavements Shopping Centre, backing on to New Beetwell Street and

Queen's Park Leisure Centre. Opened in 1987, the centre has enhanced Queen's Park with a further range of sport and leisure facilities, including a heated swimming pool.

Vicar Lane in 1987, showing the bus terminus with Hady Circular No. 5 to the fore. Most of the buildings have since been removed, one exception being the Pizza Hut (formerly John Turner's outfitters) whose mock-Tudor gabling can be seen against the skyline in the background.

fronting on the Market Place, was opened in 1981 by Prince Charles and Princess Diana. Since then the year 2000 has seen the Vicar Lane development transform the south-east end of the town, replacing various older properties with an attractively designed new complex of shops and stores. Housing along Markham Road was also demolished at the end of the 1990s, making way for a solid rank of DIY and supermarket frontages with familiar household names.

Access to out of town supermarkets like Sainsbury's off the Tapton bypass has been made easier by an improved system of road links that have largely replaced the lost railways, starting in the 1970s with the Tapton, Hasland and Dronfield bypasses, and culminating in 1985 with the main Inner Relief Road that provides a fast direct link with Chesterfield and its outlying districts. Inevitably there have been casualties. The redevelopment of Markham Road involved not only the pulling down of aged housing, but the demolition of the Queen's Park Hotel on the junction with Park Road. The Vicar Lane development has meant the disappearance of the Red Lion public house, the old 1930s bus station and the attractive St James Hall, once a venue for dancers. While on Church Lane the vicarage and its massive garden that once dominated old maps of the area now lie beneath the newly built stores. Elsewhere in the town the earth-movers have levelled much of the old Scarsdale Hospital, formerly the workhouse and Board of Guardians offices, on Newbold Road, and the same fate has befallen the Burkitt malthouse on Sheffield Road that once drew dancers as the Rendezvous Ballroom in the 1920s and '30s. Change has its price, but also provides compensations. New architecture has replaced the old, and sometimes the two fit strangely together, as with the old mock-Tudor gabling of the roof on the

John Turner store, now restructured as a Pizza Hut restaurant, on the corner of Vicar Lane and Packers Row. A few yards further on the superloo lends a space-age image that contrasts with the preserved and renovated medieval town centre. The restored shops of Low Pavement, and of Theatre and Falcon Yard, have preserved their historic identity in a modern setting. The same holds true of the Shambles, the Bowling Green, the Victorian Market Hall (now refurbished with its own covered market area) and the sloping cobbled Market Place itself, whose stalls with their bright awnings still draw the crowds on market days. Just off the Market Place, sited next to the Pavements centre, Chesterfield's new purpose-built library is very inviting. Opened in 1985 by Mark Fisher, MP, the building provides not only books but internet access, local studies, business and community information and children's services, and serves as a venue for various social and educational functions.

As with many towns, Chesterfield displays its own blend of the old and the new. The year 2000, which some regard as the dawn of a new millennium and others the end of the old one, saw the town undergoing radical change while at the same time delving into its ancient past. The year of the Vicar Lane development was also notable for the archaeological excavation of the vicarage garden on Church Way, which revealed further evidence of Roman settlement. June 2000 saw the discovery of a grave in the garden of a house on Piccadilly Road, and of a skeleton who proved to have been a priest tending to the lepers in St Leonard's hospital in the Middle Ages. The remains were reburied with a ceremony at the Spital Cemetery on 24 April this year.

As we enter the new Millennium in 2001, Chesterfield is already moving forward to embrace an unknown future. She does so from the secure base of a memorable historical past, and though much has been lost and changed, much still endures. The town's most fitting symbol is the church of St Mary's, whose crooked spire still dominates the skyline as it has done for centuries. Restored in the 1840s by Victorian architect Gilbert Scott, the church endured its own ordeal by fire in December 1961 when a fierce blaze damaged the interior, destroying the priceless Schnetzler organ, and only prompt action by the fire service prevented a worse disaster. Forty years later, St Mary's still stands, the embodiment of Chesterfield and its strength to take on the future. Like the fortunes of the town, that spire may lean from time to time, but it shows no sign of falling.

WALKING TOUR

1 The Outer Limits:

Chesterfield Old Borough Boundaries

From its origins as a medieval town in the thirteenth century to the borough extension of 1892, Chesterfield covered a small area of only 322 acres, a restriction which caused many problems in the Georgian and Victorian periods. This walk indicates the extent of the old borough, and takes in some well-known landmarks. To do so it will be necessary to cross a number of busy roads, so please take great care at all times. Also, viewing of the eastern boundary may present some difficulties for wheelchair users.

> **Start on Low Pavement in front of Boots' the chemists, facing the Market Place.**

This sloping, cobbled square was the heart of the old medieval town laid out by lord of the manor William Brewer following King John's charter of 1204, which permitted the same two weekly markets and annual fair granted to Nottingham. It replaced an earlier market place set between the parish church and Holywell Street, and is still the focal point for modern Chesterfield. Across the market place to our left can be seen the

A recent view from the parish church, showing the new shopping development.

Walking Tour

Market Hall, an Italianate-style structure built by a private company and opened in 1857; it underwent extensive improvements in the 1990s. Directly behind us is Chesterfield Library, opened by Mark Fisher, MP in 1985, and the proud owner of two awards, the RIBA architectural award and the T.C. Farries/You & Yours award for most helpful library. Beside it is the Pavements shopping centre, opened in 1981 by Prince Charles and Princess Diana during their royal visit to the town.

> **Cross the right side of the market place and turn right to enter the Shambles.**

This area is also a survival from the medieval town, and consists of buildings divided into rows which were originally used by tradesmen, mainly butchers. The name Shambles derives from the medieval 'Flescharnels' or 'Fleshambles', and refers to its use as a slaughtering area for livestock.

The Royal Oak inn occupies the site of the original medieval building, which as its sign states served as a resting-place for members of the Knights Templars (who had a settlement at Temple Normanton near Hasland) en route to their destination. The present building has undergone enlargement and alterations, and may have been entirely rebuilt in 1748, but retains much of its earlier character.

> **Turn left along Packers Row.**

Packers Row, which runs downhill past the eastern side of the Shambles, is believed to take its name from the old packhorse convoys which carried

View from the Crooked Spire, showing Stephenson Place and the view north and west.

From the Crooked Spire, the view to the east takes in the Markham Engineering site, the Inner Relief Road, and, in the distance, Hady Hill.

goods through the town, notably the salt from Cheshire which was borne along nearby Saltergate. Packers Row was also the birthplace of Emma Holmes, who as Emma Miller became famous in Australia as a leading figure in the suffragette movement.

> **At the end of Packers Row cross to Low Pavement and turn left to Falcon Yard and Theatre Yard.**

The Falcon inn (now the office of the Barnsley Building Society) is a listed building which still retains some of the original Tudor timbering. Theatre Yard once housed the old Theatre Royal which operated through the eighteenth and early nineteenth centuries, but has since been lost. These yards, with the Shambles and much of the town centre, were part of the urban decay affecting Victorian Chesterfield, but have since been restored and renovated to provide an attractive area for shoppers and tourists while ensuring their historic character is preserved.

> **Turn right and continue along South Street, cross at the pedestrian crossing and turn right again to walk down to Markham Road.**

In the early twentieth century, the area from Low Pavement to the River Hipper was occupied by slum properties from the old yards, part of which was known as the Dog Kennels. This area was cleared during the period 1911-1927, and the present road was put through in 1912. It was named after

Walking Tour

From the Crooked Spire, the view to the south-east shows the Holiday Inn and the Alma Leisure complex on Derby Road.

Charles P. Markham, head of the Staveley Company and of Markham Engineering. He was elected mayor in 1910 and, with his sister Violet Markham, took a leading role in the renewal programme. Later housing built on this side of the road was demolished in the 1990s, and the area is now taken over by the Ravenside Retail Park and the Focus Do-it-All superstore, the latter built on the site formerly occupied by the Queen's Park Hotel.

> **Use the pedestrian crossing to reach the far side of Markham Road, then turn left and walk to the end of the road, bearing right as you near the roundabout.**

From here you can see the Derby Road roundabout, formerly the 'Horns Bridge' area where three road and railway bridges crossed; Roman roadways were discovered here during reconstruction work in 1932. Horns Bridge marks the southern limit of the old borough; beyond it was the parish of Hasland.

> **Turn and retrace your steps to the crossing on Markham Road, cross and walk up to New Beetwell Street, cross by the crossing and turn right to walk to junction with Lordsmill Street. Once on Lordsmill Street, use the pedestrian crossing to reach Hollis Lane, and proceed downhill to the bridge.**

On your left, shut off by railings, is the disused railway tunnel that was once part of the Great Central Railway (Chesterfield Loop) line, one of

three railways running into the town. The line continued through the tunnel, eventually emerging at its station behind the College of Technology and Art on Infirmary Road.

Cross the footbridge above the Inner Relief Road.

Below is the Inner Relief Road opened by Dame Angela Chalker in 1985. It provides a fast direct route into Chesterfield from the north and east.

This section of the route includes two flights of steps, and may be difficult for wheelchair users. If unable to go further, it is possible to view the end of Hollis Lane as it goes over the Rother and leads to Hady Hill. If able to proceed, follow Hollis Lane past the Markham Engineering site to the bridge.

Walking Tour

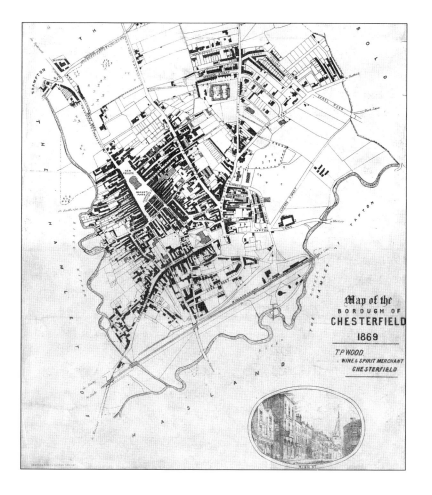

Map from T.P. Wood's Almanac of 1869, showing the boundaries of the old borough, which at this time was restricted to 322 acres.

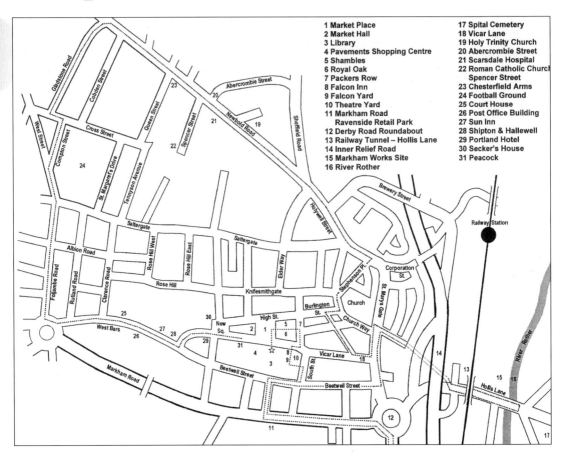

1 Market Place
2 Market Hall
3 Library
4 Pavements Shopping Centre
5 Shambles
6 Royal Oak
7 Packers Row
8 Falcon Inn
9 Falcon Yard
10 Theatre Yard
11 Markham Road
      Ravenside Retail Park
12 Derby Road Roundabout
13 Railway Tunnel – Hollis Lane
14 Inner Relief Road
15 Markham Works Site
16 River Rother

17 Spital Cemetery
18 Vicar Lane
19 Holy Trinity Church
20 Abercrombie Street
21 Scarsdale Hospital
22 Roman Catholic Church
      Spencer Street
23 Chesterfield Arms
24 Football Ground
25 Court House
26 Post Office Building
27 Sun Inn
28 Shipton & Hallewell
29 Portland Hotel
30 Secker's House
31 Peacock

Map for walk: the Outer Limits.

This part of Chesterfield runs into the district of Spital, which was formerly outside the old borough, and from the nineteenth century onwards was a home for local industries. On the right is Clayton Street, with Clayton's tannery (founded in Victorian times) at the far end. On the left is the Markham Engineering site, of which only the office buildings remain. Founded in 1889 by Charles P. Markham, the firm made tunnelling and winding equipment for the coal industry, and in recent years specialized in giant boring machines for the digging of the Channel Tunnel. Closed in 1997, the site is to become a housing estate for Shepherd Homes.

Further along to the right is the area known as Spital, where the leper hospital of St Leonard once stood, and at the end of the road is Hady Hill, with Spital Cemetery on the right hand side of the road. The River Rother marks the eastern boundary of the old borough; beyond it, Hady and Spital were part of the parish of Hasland.

Turn and retrace your steps, re-crossing the footbridge and returning to Lordsmill Street. Cross at the pedestrian crossing and walk down Vicar Lane.

*Packers Row, by George
Martin in 1964, from the
junction with Burlington
Street. One of the rows
flanking the Shambles
from the thirteenth
century onwards,
Packers Row is thought
to take its name from
the packhorse routes
through the town.*

This street, which in Victorian days was home to the Militia Barracks and
a number of old yards, has been transformed by the shopping
development of 1999-2000, which provides an attractive range of retail
outlets. Casualties have included the Chesterfield Bus Station of the
1930s, St James' Hall, the Red Lion public house and the vicarage whose
extensive garden (now built over) provided Roman remains to
archaeological excavations of 1996-2000 before the shops were erected.

> **Turn right on to Burlington Street and cross to Stephenson
> Place.**

Stephenson Place was laid out in the 1870s and named for the famous
railway pioneer George Stephenson, who is also remembered by the
Stephenson Memorial Hall on Corporation Street.

> **Use the pedestrian crossings to reach Holywell Street.**

This was one of the earliest medieval streets in Chesterfield, and was
originally known as 'Haliwelegate'. The name clearly refers to a holy well
which is believed to have been dedicated to St Helen.

> **Continue across Durrant Road.**

Durrant Road is named after the medieval land-owning Durant family, of
whom little seems to be known. Here was the location of their home

Walking Tour

Eastern wall of the Markham Works, overlooking the River Rother at Spital Bridge. The river marks the eastern boundary of the old borough.

Durant Hall, long since vanished. The site was later occupied by the old Chesterfield Royal Hospital which opened in 1859. Further back stood the Chesterfield Brewery, also established in the 1850s and since demolished.

Use the zebra crossings, and cross to Newbold Road.

One of the two main northbound roads from the town, Newbold Road led from Chesterfield to the adjoining parish of Newbold and Dunston. Ahead on the right is Holy Trinity Church, opened in 1838. The railway pioneer George Stephenson, who spent his last ten years at Tapton House east of the town, was buried here in 1848. His resting place under the altar is marked with a simple plaque inscribed 'G.S. 1848'; a stained glass window was presented to the church by his son Robert Stephenson.

A short distance further, again to the right, is Abercrombie Street, named after the Right Hon. James Abercrombie, Speaker of the House of Commons in 1835. On the left are the almost entirely demolished remains of the Scarsdale Hospital, which was built on the site of the earlier Chesterfield Workhouse and the Board of Guardians offices. The latter are the only buildings still to be preserved. Further ahead on the left is Spencer Street, and the Roman Catholic Church of St Mary and the Annunciation, opened in 1854 by the Jesuit fathers of Mount St Mary College, Spinkhill. It was the place of worship for Chesterfield's first two librarians, Dennis Gorman and George MacMahon.

Continue along Newbold Road.

Walking Tour

Ahead and to the left is the Chesterfield Arms public house, whose sign shows the arms formally adopted by the Borough in the seventeenth century, but believed to have been used much earlier. The sign shows a pomegranate tree, which in heraldic terms is 'eradicated' (torn up by the roots) and 'fructed' (bearing fruit). Why this emblem was chosen for the town of Chesterfield has still not been fully explained.

Ahead on the right are Cobden Road and beyond it Gladstone Road. Most of the streets on this part of Newbold Road are named after Liberal or reformist politicians of the nineteenth century. Newbold Road was a desirable suburban residential area in Georgian and Victorian times, and there are several good examples of houses from these periods on the road and its adjoining streets. Once at Gladstone Road you have reached the northern limit of the old borough; beyond this point lay the parish of Newbold and Dunston.

Turn left to Compton Street and continue on to Saltergate.

Saltergate is one of the original medieval streets of Chesterfield, and is believed to be the route along which packhorse trains carried their precious cargoes of salt from mines in Cheshire to the centre of town. On the corner on the left is Saltergate football ground, home of Chesterfield Football Club. Originally known as the Recreation Ground, it was in existence in Victorian times and was used for a variety of sports. W.G.

Holy Trinity church, Newbold Road. Opened in 1838, Holy Trinity is the final resting place for George Stephenson, whose grave beneath the altar is marked with a simple plaque.

Walking Tour

Grace played cricket here in 1871. (He was later to return to play twice at Queen's Park in the 1900s). Chesterfield FC reached the semi-final of the FA Cup in 1997, and in 2001 were promoted to Division Two.

> ### Cross the road and continue downhill along Foljambe Road.

Foljambe Road (formerly Pothouse Lane) is named after the Foljambe family who, from their residence in Walton, ruled as manor lords of Chesterfield in the Middle Ages. Godfrey Foljambe founded the Chesterfield Grammar School, while other family members are less pleasantly recalled for taking part in the murder of two men in and around the parish church in 1422. We are now on the western boundary of the old borough; beyond it lay the large parish of Brampton, which in the eighteenth and nineteenth centuries with its many potteries and collieries totally outmatched Chesterfield in industrial production. When Celia Fiennes commented during her visit in 1697 on 'the quarraes and the pittes of coal' lying at the end of town, these were probably in Brampton parish.

> ### Turn left and walk back along West Bars towards the town centre.

Portland Hotel, with fountain in the foreground. The fountain, brought in from Eastwood Park in Hasland, has since been removed while the hotel, built in 1904, is being redeveloped as part of the Weatherspoon chain.

West Bars marked the end of Chesterfield, and is thought to derive its name from posts or a gateway impeding entrance to the town. At one time outsiders were subject to inspection, and may have been refused admission or charged a fee to enter. This road contains a mixture of historic and modern buildings. Of the latter, the Court House on our left, the Inland Revenue building, and on the right the new Post Office administrative building (Rowland Hill House) are notable examples. Rowland Hill House, opened in 1998, replaced the Accountant General's Department (AGD) office block which employed local postal staff from the 1960s onwards. The AGD was also famous for its controversial 'Rosewall' sculpture by Barbara Hepworth. On our left is the Sun Inn, which replaces an older version. A balloon ascent was made from the yard of the Sun Inn during the 1850s. Further along and to our left are the offices of Shipton and Hallewell, solicitors established here in 1758; an excellent example of a Georgian house close to the centre of town. Ahead on the right is the former Portland Hotel, built in 1904 and soon to become a Weatherspoon house. The Lancashire, Derbyshire & East Coast Railway terminated beside the hotel, where it had its station. As the L.N.E.R. it continued to convey passengers until 1951.

Continue on to New Square.

Walking
Tour

Originally known as Swines Green, New Square was used as a place to herd livestock on market days. It was renamed in the mid-Victorian period. On the north-west corner, next to the Yorkshire Bank, is No. 87, 'Secker's House', where Thomas Secker is believed to have lived. A pupil at Chesterfield Grammar School, he became Archbishop of Canterbury in 1758.

Continue on to Low Pavement, halting at the Peacock Information and Heritage Centre.

This listed building was originally an inn, and was constructed in the fifteenth century. Now a tourist information and heritage centre, it also houses regular exhibitions, and annual well dressings take place in the old inn yard to the rear of the building. The Peacock is a fine example of a historic building being preserved and put to use in a twenty-first century context.

You have now completed your tour of the 'outer limits' of the old Chesterfield Borough.

Sun Inn, West Bars, pictured by the late Roy Stafford in 1988. This building replaced an earlier inn of the same name. In the 1850s a balloon ascent was made from the old inn yard.

Shipton & Hallewell, West Bars. A fine example of a brick-built Georgian residence in the centre of town, the building was first used by firm of local solicitors established in Chesterfield in 1758.

2 The Last Word:
Chesterfield on the Page

During its history Chesterfield has been associated with several writers, whether visitors or inhabitants. Some are household names, others less so, but all of them found something to say about the town. This walk follows in their footsteps, and recalls their voices. The walk involves the crossing of some busy roads, so please take care.

> *Start on Low Pavement facing Market Place and New Square.*

Chesterfield Market has prompted many literary responses, not least from visiting celebrities. Celia Fiennes was full of praise on her visit in 1697, when she found 'a great Market like some little faire' and was delighted with her bargain buy of 'two very good fatt white pullets for 6 pence both'. Daniel Defoe, in 1724, found most of the town unremarkable, but felt obliged to compliment Chesterfield on 'a very good market, well stored with provisions.'

In his novel *Miner* published in 1932, Chesterfield writer F.C. Boden gave a vivid and often harrowing account of a young miner's experiences during the 1926 strike. The book also contains several descriptive scenes of his native town, including a memorable picture of the Market Place and Low Pavement on a wet day in the 1920s. Local women rush to catch the Brampton tram as

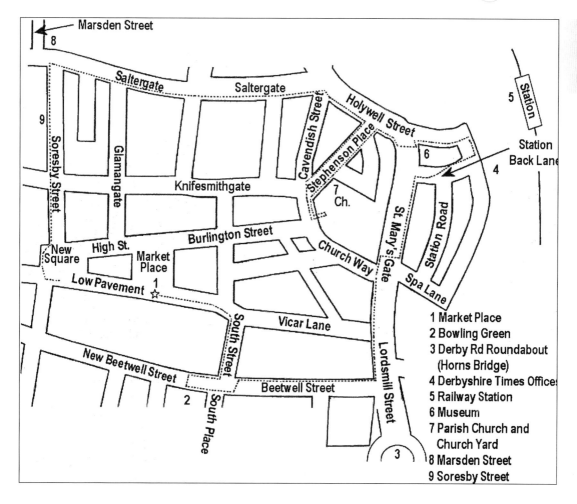

1 Market Place
2 Bowling Green
3 Derby Rd Roundabout
   (Horns Bridge)
4 Derbyshire Times Office
5 Railway Station
6 Museum
7 Parish Church and
   Church Yard
8 Marsden Street
9 Soresby Street

it arrives on High Street, and once aboard 'the whole paraphernalia groaned and rattled past the post office (on New Square), along West-Bars, and so Bramptonward.' Meanwhile: 'The west wind drove the rain in thick, slanting lines straight at the windows of shops and banks and public-houses as though it would wash them as they had never been washed before.'

More recently, in his novel *Crackin' Up* (a tale of sex, drugs and Northern Soul), Maxwell Murray uses the Market Place for an exciting motorbike chase, when Kenny, his 'mod' anti-hero is pursued past the Market Hall by a gang of leather-clad 'greasers'.

Map for walk: The Last Word.

> **Turn right and walk along Low Pavement, turning right down South Street. Use the pedestrian crossing to reach New Beetwell Street and turn left to South Place.**

Behind the high wall is the Bowling Green, believed to have been in existence since 1392. George Lee, a local tradesman, wrote a history of

Walking Tour

George Lee. A fruiterer with premises at 27 Market Hall, he was also the author of a history of the Bowling Green, and as 'Wingshaft' wrote his fictional Story of Chesterfield.

the Bowling Club in 1913 under his own name. *His Story of Chesterfield*, published around 1920 under the pseudonym of 'Wingshaft', is a fictional 'history' of the town from Celtic and Roman times to the Norman Conquest. An entertaining, bloodthirsty read with plenty of stirring speeches and epic battle scenes, it is certainly unlike any other account of Chesterfield's past.

> *Re-cross at the crossing and walk to the junction with Lordsmill Street.*

From here the Markham Road roundabout can be seen, leading to the Derby Road roundabout that was formerly 'Horn's Bridge'. Here 'Wingshaft' pictured a heroic, and entirely imaginary, battle between Celts and Romans, where Herculf the Miner defends the bridge in the manner of Horatius, hurling his adversaries to their doom before himself perishing in the fast-flowing waters.

> *Turn away from the Markham Road roundabout to face towards St. Mary's Gate. Walk up Lordsmill Street and to St Mary's Gate, crossing the junctions with Vicar Lane and Church Way, then turn right and use the pedestrian crossing to reach the opposite side of St Mary's Gate. Turn left and walk to the Stephenson Memorial Hall, stopping just short of the hall to turn right down the side road that leads on to Station Road where you face the Derbyshire Times offices.*

The *Derbyshire Times*, Chesterfield's longest-running newspaper, was founded in 1854 by Francis Augustus Hatton, who died suddenly the following year. His son Joseph Hatton later achieved fame as the editor of national newspapers, and also as a novelist. Several of his works have Chesterfield settings or episodes.

> *Turn left and continue down Station Back Lane to the junction with Corporation Street. From here it is possible to view the Chesterfield Railway Station.*

Chesterfield's original North Midland Station was built in 1840, when the line was routed along the eastern edge of the town due to the influence of railway pioneer George Stephenson. The present station is some distance further along on the same line, and has recently undergone extensive refurbishment. Violet Markham often used the station, and in *Return Passage* recalls her horror at the degraded state of the miners she saw getting off the 'paddy mail' there. This led her to campaign for improved conditions for working people in Chesterfield. More recently, Frederick Forsyth has used the modern station as a setting. In *The Fourth Protocol* his hero fells a railway porter and steals his moped to make his escape along Corporation Street and into town.

> **Walk up Corporation Street to the Stephenson Memorial Hall.**

Opened in 1879, the Stephenson Memorial Hall combined a monument to railway pioneer George Stephenson with a venue for social and educational functions. Home to Chesterfield Public Library before its move to New Beetwell Street in 1985, it is now shared by the Borough Museum and the Pomegranate Theatre. Here, on 6 October 1879, Joseph Hatton made his public reading debut, regaling his audience with extracts from his novel *Cruel London*. Hatton, whose other novels included *Three Recruits*, *By Order of the Czar*, *The Banishment of Jessop Blythe* and *A Queen of Bohemia*, often referred to Chesterfield in his work. His own life seems to have been exciting enough; as a child, he claimed to have met George Stephenson, witnessed the discovery of a murder victim's remains in the Shambles, and attended the murderer's execution at Derby. In later life he secured a 'scoop' report on the assassination of President William McKinley. Another literary inhabitant of the Stephenson Memorial Hall was George Henry Holden, librarian from 1922 to 1925. A native of Newbold, Holden left the library service in 1928 to take up a new career as a writer of articles and full-length books of recipes, fashion hints and related topics, all written under such pseudonyms as 'Inga Stromberg' and 'Ivy Priestnall-Holden' (the name of his late wife). Apparently these titles sold well in Britain, the USA and Commonwealth countries. It's unlikely anyone realized they were written by a former Chesterfield librarian!

> **Cross to St Mary's Gate using the zebra crossing, and continue right to follow the road to Stephenson Place. Walk up Stephenson Place and all the way around to the parish church and its grounds.**

Built in the thirteenth to the fifteenth centuries on the site of an older church, and greatly restored by Gilbert Scott in the 1840s, St Mary and All Saints is famous outside Chesterfield mainly for its 228 foot crooked spire, which has survived not only the centuries but severe fire damage in

George Henry Holden. He was Chesterfield librarian from 1922 to 1926, but also a successful author of beauty hints, handicraft and recipe books as 'Inga Stromberg' and 'Ivie Priestnall-Holden'.

Walking Tour

Frederick Charles Boden, poet and novelist. Raised and educated in Chesterfield, he celebrated the town in such works as Miner *and* Pithead Poems.

1961. Prior to road widening work in the 1920s when many of the graves were removed, the churchyard was much larger than it is today. Here during a visit in 1831, the Victorian novelist W. Harrison Ainsworth, author of *The Lancashire Witches* and *Old St Paul's*, felt inspired to begin his novel *Rookwood*, when 'an incident occurred, on the opening of a vault, which it is needless to relate, but which supplied me with a hint for the commencement of my romance, as well as for the ballad entitled "The Coffin".' A 'ripping yarn' in the style of Mrs Radclyffe, *Rookwood* mixes Gothic vaults and chambers, and a mysterious ancestral hall, with thrilling encounters and rescues, and manages to include Dick Turpin's ride to York in the action. One can only wonder what actually happened in Chesterfield churchyard to fire the author's imagination!

Turn back and leave the church grounds, turning right to return down Stephenson Place. Cross, using the pedestrian crossings provided, until reaching Saltergate. Continue along Saltergate to its junction with Soresby Street.

On our right is Marsden Street, and on the corner is No. 4 where the author F.C. Boden, novelist and poet, lived as a young man. Boden wrote two collections of poetry, 'Pithead Poems' and 'Out of the Coalfields', following them with the novels *Miner*, *Flo* and *A Derbyshire Tragedy*. All are based in Chesterfield and Derbyshire and contain a strong protest element, together with a frank commentary on physical relationships. Hailed by the critics, Boden later suffered unjustified neglect, but is now being read once again. It was probably this house Boden had in mind when he described Danny's visit to the pawn shop in *Miner*.

Turn left down Soresby Street.

It was on Soresby Street that Boden received what little education he could while attending the Soresby Street Council School. Like many of his generation, Boden left at thirteen to work as a miner at Williamthorpe Colliery. The school was demolished in the 1930s.

Continue down Soresby Street and return to the Market Place to end your tour.

Index